MW01017046

"WE BELIEVE": UNDERSTANDING THE NICENE CREED

Karl Przywala

Christopher Turner

Priscilla Turner

ISBN: 978-1-7751062-3-4 (sc)

C&P Books fourth printing 25/12/2023

Editor's Foreword

'Creed' is derived from Latin *credo* "I believe". It has both an intellectual and a personal sense. The Creeds are in three parts corresponding to the Three Persons of the Trinity; everyone is and always has been baptised into the Triune Name (*cf.* the Lord's instructions in Mt. 28). Creeds, as a defiant statement of faith, often in the face of other heathen beliefs, are as old as the Bible. There are quite a few in the New Testament, and they seem to be connected both with what was preached and with what new Christians were expected to stand up and say before baptism and admission to the Eucharist. The people were probably dunked three times, once after each Part.

The Apostles' Creed is the oldest Creed of any length that we have. It cannot be traced to any real Apostle, but was considered to be a fair representation of Apostolic doctrine. Like the list of New Testament books which satisfied the same criterion, it 'gelled' early in the Second Century. It formed the backbone of the great Creed of 325/451 A.D., when the Church had a big fight on its hands about the nature of Christ, and hammered out an official 'We' statement. Apart from the Athanasian Creed, these two are the only ones which date from the undivided early Church.

The age of the Creeds is very important. Guided by the Holy Spirit, the Church studied Scripture intensively and gave all Christians a sheet-anchor for ourselves in a disordered world.

We are linked by the Creeds to all our fellow-believers back through the centuries. Creeds are not the whole of our faith, but the essence of it; they are objectively true even when we don't believe a word of them. They are bigger than us. We grow into them: it has never been assumed that we must understand them completely in depth in order, say, to get confirmed. Alister McGrath writes "It may take you some time to fathom the depths of your faith". I should rather say "all the rest of your life in this world and the next".

These sermons were all delivered in Holy Trinity Anglican Church, Vancouver, BC, Canada during 2016 and 2017. I am grateful to have been asked to collate them. A minimal consistency of presentation has been imposed, while preserving each preacher's colloquialisms and other personal touches. Any other inconsistencies and errors are my own.

P.D.M.T.

Vancouver, Advent 2017.

"WE BELIEVE": UNDERSTANDING THE NICENE CREED *A SUNDAY MORNING SERMON SERIES*

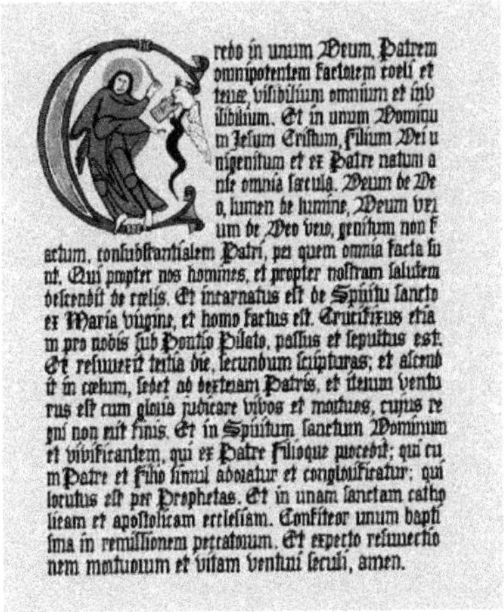
Credo in unum Deum, Patrem
omnipotentem factorem coeli et
terrae, visibilium omnium et invi
sibilium. Et in unum Dominu
m Jesum Cristum, Filium Dei u
nigenitum et ex Patre natum a
nte omnia saecula. Deum de De
o, lumen de lumine, Deum ver
um de Deo vero, genitum non f
actum, consubstantialem Patri, per quem omnia facta su
nt. Qui propter nos homines, et propter nostram salutem
descendit de coelis. Et incarnatus est de Spiritu sancto
ex Maria virgine, et homo factus est. Crucifixus etia
m pro nobis sub Pontio Pilato, passus et sepultus est.
Et resurrexit tertia die, secundum scripturas; et ascend
it in coelum, sedet ad dexteram Patris, et iterum ventu
rus est cum gloria judicare vivos et mortuos, cujus re
gni non erit finis. Et in Spiritum sanctum Dominum
et vivificantem, qui ex Patre Filioque procedit; qui cu
m Patre et Filio simul adoratur et conglorificatur; qui
locutus est per Prophetas. Et in unam sanctam catho
licam et apostolicam ecclesiam. Confiteor unum bapti
sma in remissionem peccatorum. Et expecto resurrectio
nem mortuorum et vitam venturi seculi, amen.

I: THE CREEDS – WHY "WE BELIEVE" (Karl Przywala)

During Advent, we are having a series of four sermons looking at the Nicene Creed, which we recite at Holy Communion services. I think it's good for us to have an opportunity to consider what the words we say actually mean. The series has been aired twice before – in 2011 and in the 1990s. But, in BBC-speak, don't think of this as a repeat, but 'another chance to hear'!

The Nicene Creed, being of great antiquity, was originally written in Greek, the language of the New Testament. In spite of this, our English word creed is derived from the opening word of the Latin version – *credo*. *Credo* means I believe, and that is how the Book of Common Prayer's versions of the Apostles' and Nicene Creeds are phrased – I Believe. The 1985 Book of Alternative Services retained this for the Apostles' Creed, but switched to We believe for the Nicene Creed.

At this point, I think of a parishioner in one of my former parishes, who told me he was reluctant to say we rather than I because, "I know what I believe, but I can't speak for the man standing next to me." I have some sympathy for this point of view, along with the perception that switching from I to we dilutes the emphasis on personal ownership of belief. Ultimately, we will each stand alone before Jesus as our judge, and he's interested in what's in our heart alone at that moment.

On the other hand however there's the concept that by saying the Creed, we are 'buying into' something the Church as a whole owns and promulgates. I am most aware of this when I say the third, and least often used, of our creeds – that of Saint Athanasius. The Prayer Book heads it with the Latin words *QUICUMQUE VULT*, from the opening two words, "Whoso-ever would".

Somehow, that phrase, *Quicumque vult*, instils in me a vision of what's to come. And all the more so, when we read on: "Whosoever would be saved needeth before all things to hold fast the Catholic Faith. Which Faith except a man keep whole and undefiled, without doubt he will perish eternally." Just to ram it home, after 39 verses of pretty dense theology, the Creed ends with, "This is the Catholic Faith, which except a man do faithfully and steadfastly believe, he cannot be saved." To which I find myself echoing the disciples' words in Matthew 19:25: **"When the disciples heard this, they were greatly astonished and asked, 'Who then *can* be saved?'"**

Our last Lenten Study used Diarmaid MacCulloch's video series *A History of the Christian Church*, and last Thursday morning's study group looked at the first episode again – the one in which Professor MacCulloch considers the creeds. I think this is an excellent series, and I believe that those who have seen it at Holy Trinity have found it helpful. I commend it to you; you can get the DVDs from the Vancouver Public Library, and don't let the negative review someone has posted put you off.

During her first three centuries, the Church was faced with tackling a significant question: who exactly was Jesus and what was his relationship to God? MacCulloch puts it thus: "If Jesus Christ is not fully God, then is his death on the cross enough to save you from your sins and get you to heaven? If you care about the afterlife, and they did, that's the biggest question you could ask."

The way MacCulloch phrases this, "*If* you care about the afterlife", then emphasising that this was something those early Christians did care about, suggests that others, perhaps of our time, are not so concerned about this. Why might that be? I place part of the blame with something we're all immensely grateful for, modern medicine, which has the effect of anaesthetising us, sometimes literally, from the reality of pain and death – things that those early Christians would have been much more aware of.

Why is it that in Vancouver, a proper Christian funeral service has been supplanted by something called a celebration of life? Is it because people would rather not face the reality of death, trying to pretend that the person hasn't really died? Someone told me that she thinks of her relatives as not actually having died, just 'being away on holiday.' Is it because people have given up on the idea of an afterlife, as being just so much 'pie in the sky'? Or have people bought into the idea that everyone's going to go to heaven anyway, so what's all the fuss about? The disciples had asked the question **"Who then *can* be saved?"**, as someone faced with the Athanasian Creed might do – it seems to set the bar so high, what's the chance of actually crossing it? The Philippian gaoler of Acts 16 is more positive when he asks Paul and Silas, **"Sirs, what must I do to be saved?"** [Acts 16:30]. That said, he had been about to commit suicide, thinking that Paul and Silas had escaped. Paul and Silas's answer to the gaoler's question was straightforward: **"Believe in the Lord Jesus, and you will be saved"** [v. 31]. And that is the case. That is how anyone inherits eternal life– by accepting Jesus as one's personal Lord and Saviour. But that still leaves us with the question, who is Jesus? To answer this, the early Church looked at the Bible. They looked at what Jesus said about Himself and what He did. From this they were able to assemble a picture of who Jesus is. This is who Jesus must be, in order to say these things about Himself, and be able to do these things.

Also, who Jesus wasn't – for, as you might imagine, there were plenty of spurious answers floating around, particularly before matters had been properly considered, and the creeds agreed upon and written down. Let's face it, Jesus is unique in His claim to be both God and man, so much so that He had been put to death by those who didn't think it was possible.

And some in the early Church also thought that way, coming up with what we now refer to as the heresies of Docetism – Jesus was God, but only appeared to be a man; and Arianism – Jesus was a very good man, but He wasn't actually God. The Nicene Creed settled matters, by affirming that Jesus is indeed both God and man.

Docetism's denial of Jesus' humanity is addressed when we

assert: "For us and for our salvation He came down from heaven, was incarnate from the Holy Spirit and the Virgin Mary, and was made man. For our sake He was crucified under Pontius Pilate; He suffered death and was buried." Crucially, Jesus suffered, something only a man could do.

Arianism's denial of Jesus' divinity is addressed when we assert: "We believe in one Lord, Jesus Christ, the only Son of God, eternally begotten of the Father, God from God, Light from Light true God from true God, begotten, not made."

But reading through the Creed this far still leaves a question hanging for an enquiring mind: *how* is it possible for Jesus to be both God and man, both human and divine?

The answer lies in the phrase that comes next: "of one Being with the Father." The Greek word behind "of one Being" is *homoousios* (ὁμοούσιος), which literally means 'of the same substance'; for this reason, I think that the Prayer Book's translation "of one substance with the Father" is to be preferred.

The adoption of *homoousios* made a significant contribution in helping our understanding of who Jesus is – both God and man – and how that can be. But needless to say, there were still quibbles that needed to be sorted out.

Some, led by Nestorius, Archbishop of Constantinople, held that Jesus' two natures were held much as oil and water would be in a glass – in other words, separately. Others, led by Cyril, Patriarch of Alexandria, held that the analogy is more akin to water and wine mixing.

The answer? A sort of both/and, neither or compromise between oil and water versus water and wine! The Chalcedonian Definition of 451, also sometimes referred to as a creed, states: while here on earth, Christ, the divine and human being, was recognised in two natures, without confusion, without change, but also without division, without separation. And this definition fed into the creation of our old friend, the Athanasian Creed.

The infinite monkey theorem states that a monkey hitting keys at random on a typewriter keyboard for an infinite amount of time will almost surely type a given text, such as the complete works of William Shakespeare, or indeed the Athanasian Creed. I think this theorem is bunkum!

I'd like to think that if you sat Karl down with a typewriter, or indeed paper and pen, there'd be some chance that, given enough time, a lot of time, I might come up with something akin to the Apostles' Creed. Perhaps there's a chance that I might come up with something nearing the Nicene Creed, although here you'd be stretching your Rector's grasp of theology. But the Athanasian Creed? No way, Jose!

And yet, I'm happy to recite the Athanasian Creed, and when I say I believe it, I mean what I say. In fact, when I say it, it even makes me feel quite clever: gosh, do I really believe all that!

What's going on there? It's here that I fall back upon the concept that in the creeds we are 'buying into' something the Church as a whole owns and promulgates. I accept that greater minds than mine have collectively considered these matters, even with the particular inspiration of the Holy Spirit to help them do so. And I'm willing to accept the collective wisdom that God has handed down to us through His Church.

But what about those anathemas with which the Athanasian Creed begins and finishes – aren't they a bit harsh? Here's how I get around that one. We know from Paul and Silas's answer to the gaoler's question, that if we **"Believe in the Lord Jesus ... you will be saved**." That's all that's required for salvation – accepting Jesus as one's personal Lord and Saviour. But we also know that accepting the lordship of Christ is a lifelong commitment. Who Jesus is is part of that.

As I've admitted, coming up with the Athanasian Creed is frankly beyond me, but that doesn't make Jesus any less my Lord and Saviour, nor does it make my salvation any less secure. I just accept that all three creeds, the Apostles' Creed, Nicene Creed and Athanasian Creed, are distillations of what the Bible tells us Jesus said about Himself, and what He did; and who He needs to be in order to secure my salvation, being both God and man. The crucial point is, I don't say that, having understood what a creed is saying, I then choose actively to disbelieve it. The more you understand the creeds, the richer your life in Christ will be, because you'll understand more about who Jesus is and what He has done. And I hope that this sermon series will help with that. But the bottom line is, have you accepted Jesus as your Lord and Saviour by simply saying

"Yes Lord, I believe"? If you have, then you are His and He is yours, and I look forward to seeing you on the other side.

Amen.

II: FATHER AND CREATOR (Priscilla Turner)

Texts: Gen. 1:1, 27, 31; Rom. 8:18-22; Lk. 15:11-31.

Πιστεύομεν εἰς ἕνα Θεὸν Πατέρα παντοκράτορα, ποιητὴν οὐρανοῦ καὶ γῆς, ὁρατῶν τε πάντων καὶ ἀοράτων.

"We believe in one God the Father, Ruler of all, Maker of heaven and earth and of all things visible and invisible;"

The shortest sermon I ever heard came from my firstborn, aged a bit over three-and-a-half. We were looking out of the window at the end of a long S. Ontario winter, seeing the trees beginning to bud and bloom. Slipping her soft little hand into mine, she said, "Mummy, God is kind and clever". I was very depressed at the time, having endured a personal tragedy, and I lived on that sermon for many months. I can't be as brief today: not only did I make you listen to quite a hunk of Scripture, some of whose deep things I want to remind you of, but my assignment is a few words of the Creed which encapsulate a huge area of our faith. I have written that the Creeds are based on intensive study of the Scripture. What we don't really know, apart from the enormous expansion of the Apostles' Creed which took place on the subject of Jesus the eternal Son of the Father, is exactly which texts the writers had in mind. Those that I shall cite represent some of my best guesses. You may wish to note down some of my references for yourself.

First, then, the familiar story in Lk. 15, which you may want to open now. This is Our Lord's longest parable about God as Father, and it is complete with a picture of the two main ways of going wrong in relation to Him.

The younger son is the practical atheist. He believes in God the Grandfather. To grab the loot before the old man is out of the way, and put distance between the two of them, is to take all creation for his own but treat God Himself as dead. This boy loves things and uses people for them. He is determined to live in God's world as though God Himself did not exist. He leaves to live it up and find himself; instead he gets lost and ends up as good as dead. Though he prepares a fine speech, his sense of sin is not more than knowing that, starving with the pigs (no place for a nice Jewish boy!), he's miserable. Then there's his brother. He's the RELIGIOUS type of sinner. He's never left home, but has he ever lived there? He doesn't know his father at all, or begin to understand why he still loves his younger brother, insists on loving people and using things for them. He sees his father as a slave-driver, ungenerous, legalistic and impossible to please. This man has kept all the rules, if you forget little things like love for God and neighbour. He's no better at relationships than his erring brother, with whom – "that son of yours" – he acknowledges no relationship at all. He takes a keen interest, though, in moral comparisons, in other people's sins, even to inventing what he can't know, lurid activities on which the money got spent. And he prefers to stay outside the big party rather than get mixed up with father or brother. Don't you think that the Lord means us churchy people to read him as spiritually much more calloused than his wild young brother? Last of all, there's a father who gives everything, including unqualified freedom to mess it up and reject him. For his younger son he will pine and wait for ever. He persists in treating them both as his children no matter how they treat him. When the runaway does wake up and decide to come home, he does not reproach him, but meets him more than halfway. As a middle-aged, Middle Eastern man, he does an extraordinary thing; he actually runs, for which he must hitch up his robes and make himself ridiculous. With the older one he pleads, coming out of the house himself to do it. For those hung up on God's sex, incidentally, clearly He is both father and mother; as we shall see, the composite includes someone else too.

"We believe": there are at least three ways of believing.

Firstly, there is intellectual conviction of the revealed truths of the Christian faith. I am sure that every one of us has to go through a mental housecleaning; this applies especially to those reared in non-Christian systems. The Faith is a coherent system which must be learned as a 'given', something objectively true. I say this partly because modern West-coasters are often fatally subjectivist, and we bring that baggage with us into the new life. We say that we can't believe something when we haven't experienced it, whereas there are countless wonders which we will never experience until we believe them. Many of us have come to know God in a decisive personal way; but we still need to read the Bible daily for ourselves, to submit our minds to the Word of God, learn the house-rules now that we are in God's household, and not expect some poor mortal to tell us all we need to know in 20-30 minutes once a week. This is how we become more and more at home and at rest in our believing.

Secondly, there is a personal relationship of trust, love and obedience, which is sometimes missed by those of us who have always lived, philosophically speaking, within the Christian system [*cf.* Jb. 42:5-6, where Job says that before this his knowledge of God had been hearsay, **"but now mine eye seeth thee."**]. I never myself doubted any clause of the Creed until I was twenty. I was sure that Jesus rose from the dead, but not that He was alive. Holy things can look very simple when all you do is handle the outsides of them year after year, as the elder brother did. Do not go to your grave in that state.

Lastly, there is walking in the dark and living with mystery, a mystery which grows as we grow. My personal conversion was when I gave as much of myself as I knew to as much of God as I knew. 59 years later I am amazed to realise how shallow my knowledge was both ways. I brought a shopping-list to God. Having filled it, He proceeded to see to it that everything else promptly started to go wrong. It was then that I found myself, for the first time in my life, sitting right outside my faith staring at it, and saying that it was too tall a tale. I have an analytical mind, I loathe unclarity, and walking by faith is quite unnatural to me. I am also a planner who likes to be in control. But God did not and does not explain more than one step at a time, let alone consult me. I went forward only because I couldn't go back, couldn't imagine existing without Him. No, the Christian faith is not a watertight explanation of all that happens in the world or to us personally. Faith is not knowledge, or what Scripture calls "sight". I am thinking of the whole of Job (the man never does get an explanation), I Cor. 13:8-13, Heb. 11. We are not offered that in this life. I will not pretend that I don't consider our faith easily the best explanation of why, both in the sense of "How come" and of "What for"; but we never learn more than hints about the origin of evil in the universe, technically known as the "mystery of iniquity", or have a complete answer as to how God can be perfectly loving and perfectly in control. We have to walk in the dark and live with mystery as one aspect of being creatures not the Creator. If we could get our minds around it all we should be God. To be a Christian involves trust that we have been granted sufficient understanding to go on from where we and the world are, and getting on with the job of obedience with the power He gives us.

" ... in ... God": we start from the premiss that God exists; however common practical atheism may be, *cf.* Ps. 73:11 [**"'Hogwash,' they say 'How is God going to see it? Does the Most High know anything?'"**], Rom. 1-3, the theoretical variety is as minor a theme in Scripture [**"The fool says in his heart, 'There is no God.'"** Ps. 14:1, 53:1] as it is infrequent in human experience at all times and places. Much more significant are questions, since we will all worship something, about what kind of God exists.

" ... one God": He is not an idol made by man from some component of creation (Read the brilliant polemic against idolatry in Is. 44:9-20). He does not need us. Nor is He part of a pantheon, along with the Sun, the Moon, Luck, Fate, Eros, Bacchus and so on [Ps. 82:1 *etc. etc.*]. He is not a dualism 'beyond good and evil' [**"God is light, and in Him there is no darkness at all"** I Jn. 1:5]. There is only one of Him and only He is to be worshipped [Ex. 20:3, Dt. 5:7].

" ... the Father": He is a person, not a thing to be used by us, manipulable by sympathetic magic. He will not jump through hoops for us. He has a particular character, and this is not a construct based on even the best of human parents. You and I may have had good parents, bad parents, or no parents at all; none of us had perfect parents, and neither did they; but He is the source of all that was good in them. He is relational: though the Fatherhood of God may not be twisted to mean that all of us are automatically His children, or live like it [Lk. 6:36], He is impartially good to us [Mt. 5:45]. He is full of good will, and loves His whole creation [Ps. 145:8-9] and mankind in particular [Lk. 11:11-13, 12:4-7]. If it is right to fear Him, it is definitely not because He is malignant (though Job did call Him a sadist when in his misery he touched bottom), or arbitrary. We know where we are with Him, in the sense that He means well by us and is implacably opposed to evil. The bottommost reality in the universe is personal, relational, loving and good. It follows that our individual personhood is guaranteed, even the slaves, the women and the children.

There are no unimportant people. It follows, too, that our moral sense corresponds to reality. When we hate our own sinfulness, cruelty and injustice, we can be sure that our God hates them with us, just infinitely more. In this faith we can find energy and a dynamic for change. When we fight evil, God is with us. Why, to take the example closest to home, am I a person, for whose education her earthly father impoverished himself? Why was I not sold in a cage in the marketplace by my "best before" date? Let those silly women who indict the Bible, the Fathers and the Christian faith in general for women's alleged oppression try opening their little mouths on that or any subject in any society where the Gospel has never taken firm root, and see what happens.

" ... Almighty/Ruler of all": "almighty" is not a very fortunate translation, because it sounds too abstract. It suggests among other things that He will suddenly come to from snoozing in the passenger seat, seize the wheel from us, and relieve us of the liberty He has given together with all its consequences. The Fathers meant by the word Παντοκράτωρ "all-sovereign, the governor of all". This is not a statement about our theoretical free will or determinism; it means that God is God, so that creatures/events are under His control [Ps. 104:24-30, Acts 2:23, Rom. 8:28, I Cor. 10:13]. Perhaps the most striking of those texts is Peter's statement in the Acts passage that the death of Christ was at one and the same time the responsibility of wicked men and the plan of God. We are supposed to learn to trust, not in a theory about predestination (double or otherwise), but that He INTENDED you and me, from our unique genetic makeup, through all that we would do and experience, to the moment and manner of our death. There is a point to it all, even when we can't see it. You were planned, you are in His hands, He knows what He is doing with you. There are no insignificant events. God's 'providence' is both complete, so that we can't fall through the safety-net of His guidance for us [Eph. 2:10] in spite of all our sins and blindness (and, I might add, the amount of worrying that some of us do about getting guidance) and also wholly loving in spite of appearances [Jn. 14:5-14]. Hang onto this faith, and you will not mess with the occult. "The hidden things belong to the Lord our God." A magnificent tapestry is being woven out of all that is. I don't want to be bland about this: that the personal tragedy which I thought irreparable in this world came straight in my life a quarter of a century later does not mean that everything will, in mine or yours, and it's infinitely easier to see God's hand in things that go right, or come straight after much patient waiting, than in the many hard and bitter unresolved experiences which come to us all. But what will you? Try to cut your losses and leave the Lord behind? Only the eyes of faith will see pruning [Jn. 15:2] and discipline [Heb. 12:3-13] as signs of love. The fact is that the cross, resurrection and character of Jesus are easily our main grounds for believing in God as a loving and generous Father [II Cor. 5:18 ff., I Jn. 4:7-12 *etc.*]. Jesus is pivotal: the doctrine we are considering today would never have carried conviction on the basis of a few Hebrew texts alone. Some of us have found that Jesus is never closer than when we are really going through it, and that He who asked "Why?" gives us rare glimpses of the right side of the tapestry, where the point of all the knots and crossed threads is clear.

" ... maker of heaven and earth, and of all things visible and invisible": the ramifications of this doctrine are enormous. For a start, there's no Mrs. God who has to be impregnated. Just as our God is not a fertility deity demanding to be worshipped by such foul practices as human sacrifice and ritual prostitution, He does not mate with, or share His throne with, fertility goddesses or gods. Earth, *Gaia*, is our mother only in a metaphorical sense, nor is the metaphor biblical. We are saved from the worship of something that as a deity has always proved cruel and bloody. This formulation, " ... all things visible and invisible", is elastic beyond any imaginings of the authors: it can stretch to particle physics, to the theorem which the great mathematician will say he has "discovered", not invented, to a universe so vast and old that I can't take it in, the miles of DNA in my body, time itself, that mysterious medium in which we live, even to other universes yet more complex. In this faith God is the origin of all that exists; therefore we can rely on the essential goodness of creation, including our physicality, sexuality *etc*. [Gen. 1]. Of course they are marred by sin, but they are not shattered by it. The material creation is like a superb Ming vase: it has a visible crack in it from top to bottom, but it remains glorious and God keeps it from falling apart. It is not entirely inaccurate to say that the Biblical picture of the world is of a beautiful harmony in creation, in which only the mind of man is corrupt [*cf.* Gen. 3]. I remember seeing a part of the brilliant Da Vinci's notebooks, with detailed drawings for a submarine. He wrote that he would never publish his design, because "the evil heart of man would lead him to use it in warfare". We are talking of a God out of Whose mind all matter came, and Who, perhaps not coincidentally, was incarnate as a craftsman, creating beautiful and useful things. This rules out a very old and still popular explanation of what is wrong with us, namely that we are a pure spirit imprisoned in an evil body like gas in a dirty bottle. σῶμα σῆμα, said Plato, "our corpus is our casket": the Christian view is clean contrary. We must not fear our bodies, or the sexedness apart from which we never know another adult person: a man must accept the rightness of his having and using superior size and strength to protect and provide, the beautiful young girl must not starve herself, terrified to bud and bloom, but "suffer herself to be desired/And not blush so to be admired". It is belief in a falsehood, ironically when marriage has never been more equal, childbirth safer or contraception more reliable, that spawns these perverted fears. In this faith we get ourselves into proportion: we are very small in the hands of a great God, Who made things older and bigger than ourselves [Jb. 38:4-20] as well as spiritual beings stronger than we [Heb. 1].

"God is kind and clever". Do you believe that for yourself? Will you, if you never have, come home to your Father now? Maybe you don't remember leaving; but I promise you that you will recognise Him, and to know Him will be like coming home for good. You will never be at rest anywhere else. I can't tell you what it will mean: maybe indescribable joy, maybe unspeakable suffering. Certainly you will live more intensely. Only you can choose this; you must see where you have gone wrong, yourself decide to join the party. In Jesus, God sheds His dignity. He weeps and waits, runs towards you, begs you to come in. Rom. 8:18 ff. seems to be saying that the whole sorrowing creation is waiting for you and me to do just that. I cannot prove to you that death and decay, microbes and parasites, drought, earthquake and volcano, disappointment and tragedy, appalling neglect and deliberate atrocity are not the real face of God. I do know that I see another face when I look at Jesus Christ. In this faith I hope to die.

It was on a Friday morning that they took me from the cell,
And I saw they had a carpenter to crucify as well.
You can blame it onto Pilate, you can blame it on the Jews,
You can blame it on the Devil, but it's God I accuse.

"It's God they ought to crucify, instead of you and me",
I said to the carpenter a-hanging on the tree.

"You can blame it onto Adam, you can blame it onto Eve,
You can blame it on the apple, but that I can't believe.
It was God that made the Devil, and the woman, and the man,
And there wouldn't be an apple if it wasn't in the plan."

"It's God they ought to crucify, instead of you and me",
I said to the carpenter a-hanging on the tree.

"Now Barabbas was a killer, and they let Barabbas go,
But you are being crucified for nothing here below;
And God is up in Heaven, but He doesn't do a thing,
With a million angels watching, and they never move a wing."

"It's God they ought to crucify, instead of you and me",
I said to the carpenter a-hanging on the tree.

"To hell with Jehovah," to the carpenter I said.
"I wish that a carpenter had made the world instead.

Goodbye and good luck to you: our ways they will divide.
Remember me in Heaven, the man you hung beside."

"It's God they ought to crucify, instead of you and me",
I said to the carpenter a-hanging on the tree.

(*Friday Morning*, *Songs of Faith and Doubt* by Sidney Carter 1915–2004)

III: JESUS: SON OF GOD (Christopher Turner)

Texts: Prov. 8:1, 22-31; Col. 1:15-20; Jn. 9:1-41.

Καὶ εἰς ἕνα Κύριον Ἰησοῦν Χριστόν, τὸν Υἱὸν τοῦ Θεοῦ τὸν μονογενῆ, τὸν ἐκ τοῦ Πατρὸς γεννηθέντα πρὸ πάντων τῶν αἰώνων, φῶς ἐκ φωτός, Θεὸν ἀληθινὸν ἐκ Θεοῦ ἀληθινοῦ, γεννηθέντα, οὐ ποιηθέντα, ὁμοούσιον τῷ Πατρί· δι' οὗ τὰ πάντα ἐγένετο.

"and in one Lord Jesus Christ the only-begotten Son of God begotten by the Father before all worlds, God from God, Light from Light, real God from real God, begotten not made, having the identical nature as the Father; through Him (the Son) **all things were made."**

Col. 1:15 He is the image of the invisible God, the firstborn
over all creation. 16 For by him all things were created: things
in heaven and on earth, visible and invisible, whether thrones
or powers or rulers or authorities; all things were created by
him and for him. 17 He is before all things, and in him all things
hold together. 18 And He is the head of the body, the church;
He is the beginning and the firstborn from among the dead, so
that in everything He might have the supremacy. 19 For God
was pleased to have all his fullness dwell in him, 20 and
through him to reconcile to himself all things, whether things
on earth or things in heaven, by making peace through his
blood, shed on the cross.

Today we are looking at the first few lines of the second paragraph of what we call the Nicene Creed. If we compare this with the Apostles' Creed, the first thing that strikes us is that nearly all of it is new. So I shall be trying first to explain why this chunk has been added; secondly where it has come from; and thirdly what has it got to do with us today?

The opening words are the only words that are there also in the Apostles' Creed: "We believe in one Lord Jesus Christ". And, in a sense, they are the most important words here. Not only do they establish who we are talking about, they also get us right down to the bedrock of what we believe about Him. We are talking about a man called Jesus: for his disciples and the earliest Christians this was the carpenter from Nazareth, this was the man with whom they had walked and talked for a couple of years, the man whose teaching they had heard, whose life – and death – they had observed, whose body they had handled – he was a concrete, earthy individual. Yet one whom they had recognised as the Christ, as God's anointed one, the promised Messiah. Moreover, him – and him alone – they had learned to call Lord in the full sense of the term. To call Jesus "Lord" was either arrant blasphemy or the simple truth. Throughout the Old Testament "Lord" is the title of God alone; throughout the Old Testament He declares that **"I am the Lord your God ... You shall have no other gods but me".** Then along comes a carpenter and says things like: **"Anyone who loves his father or mother more than me is not worthy of me; anyone who loves his son or daughter more than me is not worthy of me."** Do you love your parents, or your children? Do you love them more than you love the carpenter from Nazareth? Who is this Jesus who thinks that he can make demands like that? In the Gospels we find him called by Thomas **"My Lord and my God"**; and in the first Christian sermon recorded in the book of Acts Peter concludes that **"God has made this Jesus ... both Lord and Christ"**. This identification of the man Jesus with the one Lord God was a shocking blasphemy for any self-respecting Jew, yet many accepted it as the simple truth. It was a blasphemy for which Jesus Himself and many others, beginning with Stephen, were executed. We too stand by it when we say this Creed, and for us too to declare that "Jesus is Lord" is potentially a scaffold.

Why, then, do we need all this extra stuff about "the only-begotten Son, begotten from the Father before all ages, God from God, light from light, true God from true God, begotten not made, of the same being as the Father, through whom all things were made"? The immediate reason for this addition to the Creed is a negative one – to deny heretical theories; the wider reason is a positive one – because this is the kind of Christ to whom the Scriptures bear witness. Formally, only one of these phrases was a negative one: Jesus was "not made" in the way that you and I are: we are contingent creatures and, as we get on in life, our aches and pains, our loss of hearing, sight and mobility, let us know all the more certainly just how subject we are to the created order. But in fact all of this section of the Creed was put there as a kind of negative – to say "no" to the heresy that makes too little of Jesus, a false teaching that was going to recur later and is actually quite familiar to us today. Nowadays we often hear that Jesus was a good man, a great teacher, maybe even a prophet, but not intrinsically different from you and me, not what one might call God. Not long ago I read in the *Times* that in Britain there is (I quote) "pressure on the government to change guidelines on school assemblies that endow Jesus Christ with 'a special status'." The early heretics were prepared to grant a "special status" to Jesus Christ, but they still jibbed at making Him out to be fully divine, or at least divine in the same way as the Father is divine. Their slogan was "There was a time when he wasn't there", meaning that the Son was *secondary* to the Father and so did not share all the qualities of the Father. Some time later we are told that argument about the nature of Christ had become so popular and so intense that you couldn't go for a haircut without having one theory or another rammed down your throat. That is not often the topic of conversation when I go for a haircut nowadays; but I guess that the nature of our Saviour is rather more important than the question of whether the HST will be endorsed in BC or who will win the Stanley Cup. Perhaps it would not be a bad thing if we could get everyone arguing about the nature of Christ again. The Creed is concerned to establish the limits of any such dialogue, to define the minimum of Christian belief and proclamation about Jesus of Nazareth. It is a valuable part of our equipment to argue about Jesus Christ and to proclaim His Gospel. I was impressed a few years ago when our friends who came to this parish from the diocese of Singapore told us that the home groups based on the cathedral there, when they met, always said the Lord's Prayer and recited the Creed together, as if to establish a basis for their discussions and activities. Certainly the Anglican Church in Article VIII of its XXXIX Articles holds all three Creeds as to be "received and believed." And the Nicene Creed in particular is said by an expert in the field to be "the only one for which ecumenicity, or universal acceptance, can be plausibly claimed."[1]

The part of the Creed that we are looking at today is a series of hammer-blows knocking nails into the theory that "there was a time when he wasn't there" and all that it implies. He – and He alone – is not made but "begotten": "begotten" is an inescapable metaphor, one that is frequently used by St. John, telling us essentially that the relationship between the Son and the Father is something a lot closer than the relationship between something made and its maker. He is, moreover, "begotten from the Father", *i.e.* He has inherited His genes from the Father and is very like Him. I would have been tempted to title this sermon "Like Father, like Son", but even that would have been much too weak an expression for what the Nicene Fathers wanted to say through the word "begotten". In fact it seems that the original Nicene Creed added a "that is" clause at this point of the Creed, explaining that "begotten" means

[1] J.N.D. Kelly, *Early Christian Creeds* p. 296.

"from the substance/being of the Father". So that it would be a more accurate image, if cruder and not without its deficiencies, to call Jesus a "chip off the old block" since a chip is composed of the same substance, the same chemical elements in the same proportions, as the block from which it comes.

Further, Jesus is begotten from the Father "before all ages", *i.e.*, like the Father, He is outside of time – like the Father, He can claim that "before Abraham was, I am"; so that in the first chapter of his letter to the Colossians Paul can write simply that "He is before all things"; and in the *Te Deum,* we duly acknowledge Him not just as the Son of the Father but as "the *everlasting* Son of the Father". He is "God from God, light from light, true God from true God". All of these are, of course, divine titles that are being attributed to both the Father and the Son; and the little word "from" (or of/out of) says much the same as does the word "begotten": that the nature of the Son comes from and is identical with the nature of the Father. But especially the last title was aimed at the heresy that would allow Jesus to be called "god" in a subordinate way, as it were, "god" with a small letter perhaps, but certainly not "true or real God" in the sense that the Father was God. The heretics liked to point out that Jesus Himself had prayed in these words: "Now this is eternal life, that they may know thee, the only true God" (and I use the singular pronoun "thee" instead of "you" to emphasize the singularity of the "only true God"); here "the only true God" has to mean the Father. But St. John, who records that prayer, also at the end of his first epistle picks up Jesus' words and applies them to Jesus Himself, writing that "*He* (Jesus) is the true God and eternal life". He is true God from true God.

Finally we come to the most contentious clause of this Creed: "of the same being or substance as the Father". To begin with it was a contentious clause for two reasons: firstly, it was a word that was not to be found in Scripture (and incidentally we may note how concerned the Church Fathers were that all Christian dogma should be scriptural); and, secondly, it was a word that was about as ill-defined and ambiguous as are our various English versions of it. But what it came to mean was that the Son shares the same being/ substance/ essence/ nature/ character as the Father, so that, as St. Athanasius said and as is implied by the Athanasian Creed (that you can find towards the end of the BCP), "whatever is predicated of the Son is predicated of the Father". Whatever you say of the Father, you can also say of the Son; and right away the Creed gives us an example of this by declaring Jesus the agent through whom all things were made, for "by Him (as St. Paul tells the Colossians) all things were created: things in heaven and on earth, visible and invisible". There is a tremendous irony in the line from the song that Priscilla quoted last week; "I wish that a carpenter had made the world instead;" for what Paul is saying and the Creed is asserting is precisely that the carpenter on the cross is the one by whom everything was made.

The Nicene Creed takes seriously Paul's further assertion that **"God was pleased to have *all His fullness* dwell in Him"** and also Jesus' own great claim that **"I and the Father are**

one". What we profess when we say this part of the Creed is that the man Jesus is also the eternal God, as Chas. Wesley puts it in one of his hymns: "Our God contracted to a span, Incomprehensibly made man". So that the love, the mercy, the grace, the faithfulness, the wisdom that we have learnt with our minds to attribute to the Father – we actually see in the Son; and, conversely, what we see in the Son, we recognise to be the nature of the Father too.

Well, all this sounds pretty fine and, in fact, quite a magnificent piece of rhetoric; but just because it is so magnificent it seems to be far removed from us, from our everyday lives and the world of the internet and social networking. Why should *we* be interested in what a group of old fogies (many of them bishops), what *they* thought about the relationship between the Father and the Son outside of time? What does it matter to you and me today, what does it matter that we should recite this or any other creed regularly every Sunday? The short answer to this question is to tell you to come back next week, when we shall be looking at what happened after the first Christmas when He who is beyond time entered into our historical time. But I can, I think, offer one or two longer answers now. There is, for instance, something odd about Christians who persist in asking "What's in it for me?" Asking that sort of question may be how we first became Christians; but the time comes when we need to assert the truth simply because it *is* the truth. In fact, the time may well come when we need to assert the truth even to our personal disadvantage and hurt. This doctrine that the carpenter of Nazareth is of the same being as the one true

God is not something that was thought up by a bunch of old fogies a long time ago to dazzle us but to leave us essentially untouched. It is a truth to be maintained because it is based on the testimony of men like Paul, who was not one to abandon lightly his ancestral beliefs for a new-fangled Christianity, or the testimony of the writer to the Hebrews, who calls Jesus **"the exact representation of (God's) being"**. It is based on the testimony of those who knew Him intimately: John, the beloved disciple, calls Him **"the only-begotten Son who is in the bosom of the Father"**; Peter calls Him **"both Lord and Christ"**, and Thomas, the hard-to-convince, sceptical Thomas, calls Him **"my Lord and my God"**.

A second longer answer to these questions of the relevance of the Creed is that the Apostles testify not only to what He *is* but also to what He *does*. In our original text from Paul's letter to the Colossians we read that through this **"image of the invisible God, (this) firstborn over all creation ... all things are reconciled to Himself ... by making peace through His blood shed on the cross; ... Once you were alienated from God** (Paul continues) **... but now He has reconciled you"**. The apostolic testimony is that through the blood of this same carpenter from Nazareth God has reconciled all things to Himself: He has made peace, He has broken down our alienation from God, He has reconciled us; He offers us a new quality of life, a new dimension to life, a new relationship with our Maker and Lord. What's more, Jesus does what He does because He is what He is; hence the vital importance of what He is. The "blessed assurance" of which the well-known hymn speaks is based not on a psychological trick, but on the fact that there can be no fault, no blemish, no deficiency in our salvation precisely because it is wrought *not* by some kind of secondary being but by God Himself. The Creed asserts His full divinity so that it can also proclaim our full salvation. The Christian faith, the faith of the Creeds has much more to offer us than has the internet. “Begotten of the Father before all ages”, outside of time, He came into our time/our history, He came into our world, He came for our salvation – and He is God.

Perhaps more than anything else in the Creed today’s section calls us to worship. We can respect and admire a good man, a great teacher, even a prophet; but we don’t *worship* them. Today’s section spells out the fact that the carpenter from Nazareth deserves our *worship*; because He is so much more than the carpenter of Nazareth. The distinctive Christian belief is that He is the Son of God: “Veiled in flesh the Godhead see / Hail the incarnate Deity.” Paul (in the Colossians passage) says that He is to have the supremacy/the pre-eminence, and that all things were created not only *by* Him but also *for* Him. *We* are created *for* Him: the purpose of the lives that we have been given is to love Him, to serve Him, above all to worship Him. Let us do just that as we sing a hymn that was written not long after the Council of Nicaea and that is clearly inspired by these lines of the Creed defined at Nicaea, “Of the Father’s love begotten ... ”

IV: JESUS: SON OF MAN (Karl Przywala)

Texts: Dan. 7:13-14, Ps. 8, Jn. 1:1-14.

Τον δι’ ἡμᾶς τοὺς ἀνθρώπους καὶ διὰ τὴν ἡμετέραν σωτηρίαν κατελθόντα ἐκ τῶν οὐρανῶν καὶ σαρκωθέντα ἐκ Πνεύματος Ἁγίου καὶ Μαρίας τῆς Παρθένου καὶ ἐνανθρωπήσαντα. Σταυρωθέντα τε ὑπὲρ ἡμῶν ἐπὶ Ποντίου Πιλάτου, καὶ παθόντα καὶ ταφέντα. Καὶ ἀναστάντα τῇ τρίτῃ ἡμέρᾳ κατὰ τὰς Γραφάς. Καὶ ἀνελθόντα εἰς τοὺς οὐρανοὺς καὶ καθεζόμενον ἐκ δεξιῶν τοῦ Πατρός. Καὶ πάλιν ἐρχόμενον μετὰ δόξης κρῖναι ζῶντας καὶ νεκρούς, οὗ τῆς βασιλείας οὐκ ἔσται τέλος.

“For us men and for our salvation He came down from heaven, and was enfleshed through the Holy Spirit from the Virgin Mary, and was made human. He was crucified also for us under Pontius Pilate, He suffered and was buried. The third day He rose again in accordance with the Scriptures. He ascended into heaven, and is seated at the right hand of the Father. He will come again with glory to judge the living and the dead. His kingdom shall have no end.”

During Advent we’re having a series of four sermons on the Nicene Creed. I started off with a general overview. Then we looked at God the Father, and last week, Jesus’ divinity. It’s appropriate that, as we approach Christmas, we should now turn, as the Creed does, to Jesus' humanity.

But before we go any further, I want us to consider what this document is that we dutifully recite at Holy Communion, and today at Morning Prayer, because I'm preaching on it.

The Creed was written in Greek by 318 bishops who attended the first ecumenical council, held at Nicaea, in modern-day Turkey, in the year 325, under the auspices of the first Christian Emperor – Constantine. It was amended at the second ecumenical council of 381, held in Constantinople – modern-day Istanbul.

The point I want to make is that the Nicene Creed is of great antiquity, having been handed down to us across the ages. It dates back to when the Church was united as one. It is, of course, a crystallisation of doctrine that preceded it; it's not as if these things were not believed before they were written down. But it is a document that is succinct and that everyone agreed upon. We can trust it – we monkey with it at our peril.

When I was at school, I had to précis documents: to pare them down to their essentials. Perhaps that has led me to be frustrated with people who pad out what they have to say, or use words inaccurately. You can't say that of the creeds. Every word has been pored over before being agreed upon; no word is superfluous. It doesn't lend itself to being précised – it is a précis.

Therefore, when you say the words of the Creed, every one of them has meaning, is there for a purpose. If that meaning isn't obvious to you, it's worth delving deeper and considering why something is said, and why it is said the way it is. I hope that this sermon series helps with that.

If you struggle with what this thing Christianity is about, the first thing to know is that it's about Jesus. Christ – the first part of the word Christianity – is not so much a name as a title – it comes from the Greek form of the Hebrew word Messiah; so Christ and Messiah are in fact the same. Really, Jesus Christ is short for Jesus the Christ, or Jesus who is the Messiah. Some Jews who are Christian prefer to use the term Messianic Jews. They are Jews who accept that Jesus is the Messiah – the hallmark of being a Christian.

But beyond that, it's helpful to have a sketch in your mind of Jesus' life and ministry. And that's what the part of the Nicene Creed we're looking at today provides. Jesus was born as a human being, but in a special way. He was put to death by crucifixion and then rose back to life from death. He returned to heaven, which is where He is until He comes back to earth again. There you have it: the Incarnation, Crucifixion, Resurrection, Ascension, and Second Coming. Get those five events clear in your mind, and you'll have something to talk about when next you have opportunity to share what it is you believe.

Let's look a little closer at how the Nicene Creed expresses these things. "Who for us men and for our salvation." Remember what I said about monkeying with the Creed? This is something that's been monkeyed with in modern liturgies!

Those who wrote the Creed used the Greek word *anthrōpous,* (ἀνθρώπους) from which we get our word anthropology, meaning the study of mankind. They could have left this word out and said, "for us", as modern liturgies tend to. But they didn't, and they didn't for a reason. Just saying "us", leaves hanging the question of who the "us" is. Is the "us" we who are assembled in a particular place? Is it all who are professing Christians? The answer is no to both of these, or at least it's yes, but not only. Jesus came down from heaven, and was made **man** (ἐ**νανθρωπ**ήσαντα, a term which appears to be a Christian coinage), in order to offer salvation to *all* mankind.

Some contemporary worship songs are bad in terms ofmusic, more often nowadays not because of the triteness that exemplified some earlier songs, but because they're just too complex for congregational singing; they're designed to be performed rather than joined in with. But some songs have excellent music, but fall down when it comes to their theology– they're just not biblical.

I put the song 'Above All' into this category. There's what some consider a minor Karl quibble: "You lived to die, rejected and alone." Jesus didn't die alone: there was a long list of people who witnessed His death, including the two thieves crucified alongside Him.

But more seriously perhaps, there's this line about Jesus' death: "You took the fall and thought of me above all." I don't claim to know what was going through Jesus' mind as He died. Maybe He thought about His death's being, as the Prayer Book puts it, "for the sins of the whole world"; but I'm pretty sure that He wasn't 'thinking of Karl Przywala above all'!

Sometimes Jesus' death is thought of as a tragedy. In one sense it was: tragic and painful. But, alongside this, we need to put that Jesus' death was necessary and inevitable. The Creed says as much: Jesus "came down from heaven", "for us men and for our salvation." And the way that He achieved our salvation was through His death. He was the man who was born to die – in a specific preordained way, and for a specific preordained purpose.

"And was incarnate by the Holy Ghost of the Virgin Mary." Jesus' birth was special. The fact that Mary was a virgin shows that it was so. The Creed tells us how this was brought about: "by the Holy Ghost."

"And was made man." This contrasts with what we've said about the Lord Jesus Christ, earlier in the Creed: "Begotten, not made." How do we reconcile these two statements? The link is, "came down from heaven." The Lord Jesus Christ, as the second person of the Trinity, pre-existed His birth. It's in this sense that He was "Begotten, not made." Incarnate means "made flesh", and the flesh in which the second person of the Trinity was embodied was that of a man – the same as you and me.

"And was crucified also for us under Pontius Pilate." The Creed had already established who the "us" is for whom Jesus was crucified: all mankind. But Stuart Townend's song 'How deep the Father's love for us' introduces a more appropriate sense of 'me-ism' than is found in the song 'Above All', when he writes:

> Behold the Man upon a cross,
> My sin upon His shoulders
> Ashamed I hear my mocking voice,
> Call out among the scoffers
> It was my sin that held Him there
> Until it was accomplished …

An essential part of becoming a Christian is to reach a point of realisation that Jesus died for you, for your sin: It was my sin that held Him there. We're reminded of this at the distribution of the bread and wine at Holy Communion:

> The body of our Lord Jesus Christ, which was given for thee ... Take and eat this in remembrance that Christ died for thee.

> The blood of our Lord Jesus Christ, which was shed for thee ... Drink this in remembrance that Christ's blood was shed for thee.

The use of the singular 'thee' rather than the plural 'you' emphasises that as well as Jesus' death being "for the sins of the whole world", it also calls for an individual response of faith: "feed on him in thy heart by faith."

I have made the journey to the Holy Land once. When I was in the town of Caesarea, it was interesting to see a stone inscribed with the name of the Roman governor: Pontius Pilate. Reference to Pilate is made in the Creed for the sake of historical verification. He was a real historical person in the way that Jesus was. But regarding who was ultimately responsible for Jesus' death – the Romans, the Jews – as good an answer as any is you and me, through our sin.

"He suffered and was buried." Jesus was a man, like you and me, and He suffered, just as we would, if we were put through what He was physically. And you don't bury someone who isn't dead: "Sealed in the stone-cold tomb."

"And the third day He rose again according to the Scriptures." This line in the Creed is a direct lift from I Corinthians 15, where Paul writes in verses three and four: **"Christ died for our sins according to the Scriptures ... he was buried** (and) **He was raised on the third day according to the Scriptures."**

Here, the Book of Alternative Services' wording "in accordance with the scriptures" has something to commend it. It isn't that the Bible says that Jesus rose, but, well, we're not so sure. But rather that Jesus' resurrection was a fulfilment of biblical prophecy, such as Ps. 16:10, **"You will not abandon me to the grave, nor will you let your Holy One see decay."**

"And ascended into heaven, And sitteth on the right hand of the Father." Christ had come "down from heaven." Forty days after his resurrection, He returned there. But there was now an unalterable difference. He had been "made man" and that fact was not undone by his death or resurrection. And so He took his humanity, including a resurrection body akin to the one we will have, with Him into heaven.

The Ascensiontide hymn 'Hail the day that sees Him rise' expresses this:

> Him though highest Heaven receives,
> Still He loves the earth He leaves,
> Though returning to His throne,
> Still He calls mankind His own.
>
> See! He lifts His hands above,
> See! He shows the prints of love – *being the wounds in His hands from his crucifixion*
> Hark! His gracious lips bestow,
> Blessings on His church below.

To sit "on the right hand of the Father" is to be put in the place of highest honour. We're familiar with this concept from formal meals, where the guest of honour sits to the immediate right of the host.

"And He shall come again with glory to judge both the quick and the dead: Whose kingdom shall have no end." Each time we sing in the *Te Deum*, as we have done today, "We believe that thou shalt come to be our judge", I feel a pang of shame. I recall how a foolishly sproggy Karl once suggested that reference to Jesus' second coming wasn't required in a statement of faith. Well, I've repented of that error – more evidence of why it's best not to monkey with the Creeds.

I believe that Miles, our onetime Musician in Residence, may in the past have come in for some ribbing over the fact that Jesus' purpose will be to judge the quick – his surname is Quick. His response is that perhaps it's better to be quick, i.e. living, rather than the alternative!

As Christians, God's people, we live as part of God's kingdom currently. But even as we do so, we're aware of our failings, and the failings of the world that surrounds us. We look forward to a time, heralded by Jesus' return, when all will be as God intends, which goes for us and what will surround us.

His kingdom cannot fail,
He rules o'er earth and heaven;
The keys of death and hell
Are to our Jesus given.

Rejoice in glorious hope!
Our Lord and judge shall come
And take His servants up
To their eternal home:
Lift up your heart,
Lift up your voice!
Rejoice, again I say, rejoice!

Amen.

V: CHRIST'S RETURN (Karl Przywala)

Texts: I Thess. 4:13-18, Mt. 24:36-51.

Καὶ πάλιν ἐρχόμενον μετὰ δόξης κρῖναι ζῶντας καὶ νεκρούς, οὗ τῆς βασιλείας οὐκ ἔσται τέλος.

"And He will come again with glory, to judge both the living and the dead; his kingdom will have no end."

When I was at theological college in Australia, a friend was much perturbed because the bishop of the diocese where he was due to be ordained had said that he thought that Christ's return had already happened. The idea espoused by the errant bishop was that this had occurred with the coming of the Holy Spirit at Pentecost.

Should I be pleased at this novel concept? It does, after all, appear to give a fillip to the so-called *filioque* clause[2] , of which I am an advocate – "the Holy Spirit ... proceeds from the Father *and the Son.*" Yes, we may refer to the Holy Spirit as the Spirit of Jesus.

But I wanted to ask the bishop (no names, no pack drill!), how

---

[2] Not original, but added later into the Latin text of the Nicene Creed. It originated in Spain, and was not officially adopted by Rome for several centuries.

he felt about the Holy Communion service, which is referred to as "a perpetual memorial of (Jesus') precious death, *until his coming again.*" If Jesus had already returned, why do we still administer Holy Communion?

More straightforwardly, I could have asked him why we say in the Creed that Jesus "*will* come again" – future tense. The Nicene Creed was written three centuries after the coming of the Holy Spirit at Pentecost. Yet the bishops who wrote it clearly viewed Jesus' return as a future rather than past event.

The Creeds are subordinate standards of doctrine. They are subordinate to the Bible, as what they contain is derived from the Bible – they are summaries of essential biblical teaching. Article VIII of the XXXIX Articles of Religion makes this clear: "(The Creeds) ought thoroughly to be received and believed: for they may be proved by most certain warrants of holy Scripture."

Please turn to our passage from I Thessalonians, which you'll find on page 1148 of the church Bibles, I Thessalonians chapter 4, beginning at verse 13. Paul is writing, after the Pentecost event, about Jesus' return, and it's clear that it's yet to occur. Verse 16: **"the Lord Himself *will* come down from heaven"** – future tense.

Yet I Thessalonians was written nearly 2,000 years ago. That leaves plenty of time for Jesus' return to have occurred between then and now. After all, Jesus did, somewhat enigmatically, say that **"some who are standing here will not taste death before they see the Son of Man coming in his kingdom"**, Mt. 16:28. And Paul talks in verse 15 of our I Thessalonians passage of us

"who are still alive, who are left until the coming of the Lord."

Earnest Christians, perhaps drawing upon the Parable of the Sheep and the Goats in Matthew 25, **"Lord, when did we see you ... and did not help you"** [v. 44], sometimes fret, what if Jesus has returned and we haven't recognised Him?

Jesus' first coming, being born at Bethlehem, had its spectacular aspects, but it didn't appear to have a lasting impact at the time. Jesus' disciples didn't know what to make of Him during his lifetime – they didn't recognise Him for who He was; and we ended up killing Him. Heaven forbid that something similar should happen again!

Worry ye not. Jesus' second coming will be quite different from his first. He shall return not as a newborn baby, but as an adult – He was at least 33 when He died. And it will be quite an event. Verse 16 again: **"The Lord Himself will come down from heaven, with a loud command, with the voice of the arch-angel and with the trumpet call of God."** Trumpets can be quite loud and penetrating – I've always fancied being a trumpeter! The trumpet call of God will resound throughout the world – loudly and unmistakably.

In our passage from Matthew chapter 24, Jesus compares his return with the flood at the time of Noah, with being burglarised – I must admit I'd never come across that verb until coming to Canada – and with a master's returning to find out what his servant has been up to.

I'm reminded of a Punch cartoon. Two employees are sitting at their desks. “Look busy,” one says, “it’s about time for the boss to drop by.” Behind them, through the window, we see the boss glaring at them from his hang-glider!

Anyone who has experienced a flood, if only in the bathroom, or who has been burglarised, or has been an employee who has been caught out by his boss, will know that such events are not readily missed or overlooked.

John, in his vision of Jesus’ return, writes: **“Look, He is coming with the clouds, and every eye will see Him, even those who pierced Him”**, Revelation 1:7. At our Advent service, we sang Charles Wesley’s hymn, ‘Lo, He comes with clouds descending’:

Every eye shall now behold him,
Robed in dreadful majesty;
Those who set at nought and sold him,
Pierced, and nailed him to the tree,
Deeply wailing,
Shall the true Messiah see.

We believe that Jesus “will come again in glory.”

Last Sunday, you sang the canticle *Te Deum* at Morning Prayer, as you will again on Easter Day in three weeks’ time. One of the *Te Deum*’s most resonant lines is: “We believe that thou shalt come to be our Judge.” It’s not surprising that this line is included, as the canticle follows the outline of the Apostles’ Creed, mixing a poetic vision of heavenly worship with its declaration of faith.

The subject of judgement isn't always a popular one. At last Thursday's Bible study, Ida was most concerned about the fate of the goats in Jesus' Matthew 25 parable. That said, in the Old Testament, there are often calls for God to execute his judgement; there's a pervasive feeling that the wicked get away with too much.

If we have ever been a victim, we can probably relate to a feeling that justice needs to be done. And we might resort to going before a judge for this to be so. My parents did this, taking a case before the Small Claims Court, when a driver failed to pay for the damage he had done to their car.

There seems to be plenty in the newspapers about the justice system, particularly when a judge is deemed to have failed in some way in executing his duty. If we were the plaintiff, we wouldn't be impressed if the judge were to exonerate someone who was evidently guilty.

There's a debate in some circles, about whether Christians will face judgement; perhaps on the basis of Jesus' words in John 5:24: **"I tell you the truth, whoever hears my word and believes Him who sent me has eternal life and will not be judged; he has crossed over from death to life."**

There are plenty of other places in the Bible, however, that state that Christians are not exempt from judgement by God. For example, Paul writes in Romans 4:10-11: **"We will all stand before God's Judgement seat. It is written: 'As surely as I live,' says the Lord, 'every knee will bow before me; every tongue will acknowledge God.'"**

We must always look at what the totality of Scripture has to say on a subject. Indeed, even in John 5:24, the word translated "judged" can also be translated as "condemned", which is what our 1984 version of the NIV does: **"I tell you the truth, whoever hears my word and believes Him who sent me has eternal life and will not be condemned."**

Back in October 2015, I preached on I Corinthians chapter 3. In verses 13 through 15, Paul writes: **"Fire will test the quality of each man's work. If what he has built survives, he will receive his reward. If it is burned up, he will suffer loss; he himself will be saved, but only as one escaping through flames."**

What is at stake as a Christian faces judgement is not our salvation. That is secured through our belief in Jesus as Lord and Saviour: **"God so loved the world that He gave his one and only Son, that whoever believes in Him shall not perish but have eternal life"**, John 3:16. But God is still interested in how we have spent our lives: **"Each of us will give an account of himself to God"**, Romans 14:12.

We believe that Jesus "will come again in glory to judge the living and the dead."

At the beginning of our passage from I Thessalonians 4, Paul writes, verse 13: **"Brothers, we do not want you to be ignorant about those who fall asleep."** "Fall asleep" is a metaphor for death. It's a particularly apt one for those who are Christian.

Jesus said from the cross to the penitent thief beside Him: **"Today you will be with me in paradise"**, Luke 23:43.

Paradise is the place of rest for those who are Christ's followers, between their death and when they will be resurrected. They will be there with Jesus; at Jesus' return they will be reunited with their resurrected bodies. Verse 14: **"God will bring with Jesus those who have fallen asleep in Him"**; and verse 16: **"the dead in Christ will rise first."**

Paul continues, verse 17: **"After that, we who are still alive and are left will be caught up together with them in the clouds to meet the Lord in the air."** I wonder whether this is where the popular image of eternal life being spent sitting on fluffy white clouds comes from. But "clouds" and "in the air" are only mentioned in terms of meeting Jesus, and even then, I take it, as picture-language. Revelation 21 makes it clear that there will in fact be **"a new earth"** [v. 1] for us to inhabit for eternity.

We end the Lord's Prayer with a doxology: "For thine is the kingdom, the power, and the glory for ever and ever. Amen." This echoes Gabriel's words to Mary about Jesus: **"His kingdom will never end"**, Luke 1:33.

The New Testament talks much about the kingdom of God, or the kingdom of heaven – it's the same thing. We who are Christian are currently part of God's kingdom, even if, at times, it may not feel like it.

Does anyone know the significance of the date 6th June 1944? It was D-Day – the start of the Normandy landings during the Second World War. From that date, we know in retrospect that Hitler's fate was sealed, although he didn't commit suicide until nearly a year later, with V.E. Day being 8th May 1945.

We are now living in in-between times. Yes, we who are Christian, who have accepted Jesus as our personal Lord and Saviour, are part of God's kingdom, heralded by Jesus' death, resurrection and ascension – those events being equivalent to D-Day.

But we await the consummation of this. Satan knows he's defeated, but he fights on still, until he will finally be put to death at Jesus' return. We await expectantly that final victory day. It is then that we shall see and experience God's kingdom in all its fullness and glory.

We believe that "his kingdom will have no end."

As Paul writes in Philippians chapter 2, at that time, **"At the name of Jesus every knee shall bow, in heaven and on earth and under the earth, and every tongue confess that Jesus is Lord"** [vv. 10, 11].

> Yea, amen! let all adore thee,
> High on thine eternal throne;
> Saviour, take the power and glory;
> Claim the kingdom for thine own:
> Thou shalt reign, and thou alone.

"Even so, come, Lord Jesus!" [Revelation 22:20].

Amen.

VI: THE HOLY SPIRIT (Karl Przywala)

Text: Jn. 16:5-16.

Καὶ εἰς τὸ Πνεῦμα τὸ Ἅγιον, τὸ Κύριον, καὶ τὸ ζωοποιόν, τὸ ἐκ τοῦ Πατρὸς ἐκπορευόμενον, τὸ σὺν Πατρὶ καὶ Υἱῷ συμπροσκυνούμενον καὶ συνδοξαζόμενον, τὸ λαλῆσαν διὰ τῶν προφητῶν.

"We believe in the Holy Spirit, the Lord, the Giver of life, Who issues from the Father, and with the Father and the Son is worshipped and glorified, and Who spoke through the Prophets."

We are resuming our sermon series looking at the Nicene Creed, which is why we had it as part of our service earlier. We've reached "We believe in the Holy Spirit."

That clause already tells us something about the Holy Spirit. We believe in Him. We believe many things as Christians. But what or whom do we ultimately believe in? God. We believe in God. And that is who the Holy Spirit is. He is one of the three persons of the Holy Trinity: God the Father, God the Son, God the Holy Spirit. As such, the Holy Spirit is never an 'it'; we refer to Him as 'he', one of the three persons of the Trinity.

I can remember when forms used to ask what your sex is: male or female. Now, you're more often asked what your gender is. I baulk at this, because gender refers not to people, but to those languages, roughly a quarter and not English, that have masculine and feminine grammatical categories of nouns. This is not the same, and should not be confused with, a person's sex: male or female.

It is true that in Hebrew, the language of nearly all the Old Testament, the word for spirit, *ruach* (רוּחַ), is feminine in gender, unlike in Greek – neuter, and Latin – masculine. But even given what I've said already about gender, *ruach* is a curious example, because it uses masculine grammatical forms of associated verbs. The Holy Spirit is correctly referred to as 'he', not 'she', and not 'it'.

When I talk about baptism, I tend to refer to a passage earlier in John's gospel account, when Jesus is speaking to a Jewish Pharisee named Nicodemus. Jesus tells him, **"I tell you the truth, no one can see the kingdom of God unless he is born again"**, John 3:3.

Imprinted on my memory is sitting in St. Jude's Church in October 1985, newly arrived to take up a position with Her Majesty's Inspector of Taxes, Belfast 4 District. The curate was preaching on this text, **"You must be born again."** [John 3:7], and said this even applies to members of the Church of Ireland! Wow, this is good, I thought.

All of us are born physically, and this is a gift from God. Back in Genesis we read that **"the Lord God formed the man from**

the dust of the ground and breathed into his nostrils the breath of life, and the man became a living being.", Genesis 2:7. The Hebrew words used for "breath of life" are related to the word for spirit, *ruach.*

But when Jesus says **"You must be born again"**, He's referring to being born spiritually. This doesn't happen automatically. It doesn't happen because you're English, or Canadian, or a member of the Church of Ireland or the Anglican Church of Canada. You can be any of these, and many are, without having been born again.

Jesus says, **"Flesh gives birth to flesh, but the Spirit gives birth to spirit. You should not be surprised at my saying, 'You must be born again'"**, John 3:6-7. This spiritual rebirth is brought about by the Holy Spirit: "We believe in the Holy Spirit, the Lord, the giver of life."

Please turn to our passage, which you'll find on page 1047 of the church Bibles, John chapter 16. Verse 8: **"When He** (the Spirit) **comes, He will convict the world of guilt in regard to sin and righteousness and judgement."**

I know that some of you have been to the Festival of Hope on Friday and Saturday; I hope that many more of you will be there tonight. Franklin Graham presents a clear gospel message, as did his father, Billy Graham. This does not skirt around the need for us to recognise our sin and our need of salvation as we turn to God.

On Friday, Franklin Graham illustrated this with reference to the sin of King Belshazzar in the Old Testament, Daniel chapter 5. Last night, he spoke about the sin of the prodigal son, stuck in the mire of the pigpen, Luke 15.

The Holy Spirit enables us to come to God in repentance and faith – He gives us new life in this way. We need to acknowledge the reality of sin, in the world and in our own lives personally – sin that separates us from God. To re-cognise that, as Paul says in Romans 3:10, **"There is no one righteous, not even one"**, apart that is, from Jesus, who died on the cross for our sin, yours and mine.

If you have yet to acknowledge that, perhaps tonight at the Festival of Hope will provide an opportunity to do so: to get up out of your seat and come to God in repentance and faith. If you do, it's the Holy Spirit, "the Lord, the giver of life", that's enabling that to happen.

Verse 7 of our passage: Jesus says, **"But I tell you the truth: It is for your good that I am going away. Unless I go away, the Counsellor** (that is the Holy Spirit) **will not come to you; but if I go, I will send Him to you."** It is only by the Holy Spirit that Jesus is now present in this world.

Verse 12: Jesus says, **"I have much more to say to you, more than you can now bear. But when he, the Spirit of truth, comes, He will guide you into all truth. He will not speak on His own; He will speak only what He hears."** And how will the Spirit hear it? Directly from Jesus.

Verse 15: Jesus says, **"All that belongs to the Father is mine. That is why I said the Spirit will receive from me** (Jesus) **what He will make known to you."**

That is why we may refer to the Holy Spirit as the Spirit of Jesus. Jesus, in His earthly ministry, could be in one place only at one time. Through the Holy Spirit, Jesus is with us everywhere. That is why Jesus said, **"It is for your good that I am going away. Unless I go away,** (the Holy Spirit) **will not come to you."** We may talk about Jesus living in the heart of those who are His followers, those of us who are Christian. How does Jesus do that? Through the Holy Spirit Who proceeds from Him.

The next line in the Nicene Creed says, "With the Father and the Son (the Holy Spirit) is worshipped and glorified." That is why we say, "Glory to the Father and to the Son and to the Holy Spirit" as part of our liturgies. As the Athanasian Creed puts it, "the Godhead of the Father, and of the Son, and of the Holy Ghost (another way of referring to the Holy Spirit) is all one, the glory equal, the majesty co-eternal." But herein lies a paradox.

We all know that if your main rôle is to communicate for another person, it is not appropriate to sing your own praises. And the Holy Spirit always avoids that, because what He does is exactly the opposite. Jesus says in verse 14, **"He** (the Holy Spirit) **will bring glory to *me*** (Jesus) **by taking from what is mine and making it known to you."**

Although the Holy Spirit is God and the third person of the Holy Trinity, He never draws attention to Himself. His concern is to glorify Jesus. In this, He is the ultimate exemplar of true self-effacement.

And that's how we should be in our Christian lives. The acid test of any worthwhile ministry or activity is not whether we help ourselves or even others. It's how much we bring glory to Jesus by placing Him front and centre in everything that we do.

The same is true of all that the Spirit does. It's for our good and Christ's glory. When He convicts us of sin, it is so that we can change for the better. When He communicates Christ's truth to us, it is so that we can learn and apply it. And when He glorifies Christ, it is so that we might know Christ, receive Him and give Him the honour due to His name.

Our final line from the Nicene Creed for now: "He (the Holy Spirit) has spoken through the prophets." The Holy Spirit came in a special way on the apostles in Jerusalem at Pentecost, as recorded in Acts chapter 2, something we mark on Whit Sunday. But He had not been absent before then. Indeed, he's mentioned right at the beginning of the Bible: **"The Spirit of God was hovering over the waters"**, Genesis 1:2.

It was through the Holy Spirit that the Old Testament prophets were able to bring their message from God. And the Holy Spirit continues to do this. Our contemporary versions of prophets and prophecy are preachers and sermons.

If I were to say to you that it's through the Holy Spirit that I'm able to speak to you, that would be misleading. Because, as you well know, I'm quite capable of speaking of my own accord. Let's look back at verses 12 and 13: Jesus says, **"I have much more to say to you, more than you can now bear. But when he, the Spirit of truth, comes, He will guide you into all the truth. He will not speak on his own; He will speak only what He hears."**

The Holy Spirit is active in prophetic preaching, when the preacher expounds not **"on His own"** but **"what He hears** (from Jesus)". And that is to be found in the Bible, "God's Word written" [Article XX], which is, from cover to cover, our record of God's revelation to us through Jesus.

Paul writes: **"All Scripture is God-breathed"**, II Timothy 3:16.[3] Some translations say "inspired" rather than "God-breathed", which means the same thing. But God-breathed is a good translation, because it gets us to the Greek original; the word for breath being the same as for spirit. It was through the Holy Spirit that the Bible's writers were inspired to write what they did, so making it "God's Word written."

The ministry of the Holy Spirit is rich and multifaceted. But the points that we have considered from John 16 can truly transform our lives when we take them to heart.

---

[3] His reference was of course to his Bible, the canonical Scriptures of the Old Testament; but it may be extended to those of the New Testament which were to be written.

The Holy Spirit is God: one of the three persons of the Holy Trinity. The Holy Spirit, the Lord, the giver of life, enables us to be born and to be born again, coming alive spiritually to the things of God. Coming to Him in repentance and faith, on the basis of Jesus' death on the cross for us. I hope that you have done that or are willing to do so.

The Holy Spirit tells us about Jesus, who He is and what He has done for us, particularly His death and resurrection, and enables us to give Jesus the glory: "Thine be the glory, risen, conquering Son; endless is the victory, thou o'er death hast won."

The Holy Spirit has spoken through the prophets, and continues to do so, wherever God's Word to us in the Bible is faithfully proclaimed.

Amen.

VII: THE CHURCH (Karl Przywala)

Texts: Eph. 1, Mt. 16:13-19.

Εἰς μίαν, Ἁγίαν, Καθολικὴν καὶ Ἀποστολικὴν Ἐκκλησίαν. Ὁμολογῶ ἓν βάπτισμα εἰς ἄφεσιν ἁμαρτιῶν.

"We believe One, Holy, Catholic and Apostolic Church. I acknowledge one baptism for the remission of sins."

"With regard to religion, finally, it may be briefly said that (Lucia) believed in God in much the same way as she believed in Australia. For she had no doubts whatever as to the existence of either; and she went to church on Sunday in much the same spirit as she would look at a kangaroo in the zoological gardens; for kangaroos came from Australia."

That is a quotation from the novel *Queen Lucia* by E.F. Benson. I can claim a tenuous connection, as Benson's father, Edward, went to the same school as me; the father also went on to become Archbishop of Canterbury – there the connection ends!

I'm rather glad that today is a Prayer Book service, as it makes it natural for me to quote from the Prayer Book's version of the Nicene Creed – which remains normative for Anglicans. There's a difference between the Prayer Book's version of the Creed and that found in the Book of Alternative Services.

Leaving aside the fact that the Prayer Book couches matters in the first-person *singular*, “I”, whereas the BAS uses the *plural*, “We”, the BAS inserts the preposition “in”: “We believe *in* one holy catholic and apostolic Church”, whereas the Prayer Book has “And I believe One, Holy, Catholic, and Apostolic Church.”

In doing this, the Prayer Book is following the Latin text. There’s a difference between: *credo in Deum* and *credo Ecclesiam.* The sense of the latter is “I believe the One, Holy, Catholic, and Apostolic Church.” Not, I believe that it exists, rather in the same way that Lucia believed in Australia and kangaroos, i.e. the fact that it exists has little or no impact on my life, but rather, I share in its existence, because what it stands for and teaches is part of who I am.

I have stuck in my memory bank a recollection that Rowan Williams critiqued liberal Christianity for its tendency to end up merely endorsing society’s *mores*. Having said that, I spent far too long fruitlessly searching the Internet for a quotation from him to that effect, and I’m now left wondering if my memory is at fault; what do you do if ‘computer says no’?

My memory is that the quotation is along the lines that Christianity must be more than just a coating to be sprinkled over society’s norms. If not Williams, former Archbishop of Canterbury, then perhaps someone else with a pointy hat said it. Someone more important than me, anyway!

It’s a sentiment Paul endorsed in his letter to the Romans: **“Do not conform any longer to the pattern of this world, but be transformed by the renewing of your mind”**, Romans 12:2.

I even used to have a T-shirt with this on it – it showed a fish going against the flow. It's a sentiment Paul echoes in his second letter to the Corinthians, quoting the prophet Isaiah: **"Therefore come out from them and be separate, says the Lord"**, II Corinthians 6:17.

That's what it means to be holy: to be separate, set apart for God. To say that the Church is holy is to affirm that it is set apart from the world and its ways; set apart by God for His purposes. Our English word 'church' reflects this idea. It comes from the Greek *kuriakon dōma* (κυριακόν δῶμα) meaning the 'Lord's house'. In being set apart, the Church belongs to the Lord for His purpose.

I had trouble in my last parishes, I had six of them, at the same time, with one of my wardens, I had twelve of them, when I introduced saying the 'Prayer for all sorts and conditions of men'. No, the problem wasn't the 'men' part, in fact we termed it 'Prayer for people in every kind of need'. The issue was that it included the line: "We pray for the good estate of the catholic church." Ken expostulated, "I've never prayed for the catholic church, and I'm not going to do so now!"

It's a matter of regret that good Christian words have become expropriated by particular denominations. 'Orthodoxy' has become associated with the Eastern Orthodox Churches. Yet it means 'right belief' – we are all called to be orthodox in what we believe as Christians; the alternative is to be heterodox – to have wrong beliefs.

And 'catholic' is used as shorthand for Roman Catholic, which is obviously how Ken thought of it. But 'catholic' just means universal, a word that Cranmer substituted in his 'Prayer for the Church militant', which we'll be saying shortly. In saying "I believe the One Catholic Church", what we mean is, I'm part of a Church that exists throughout, and beyond, time, and in all places. At the Reformation, the Church of England was clear that it was the valid expression of the Catholic Church at that time: "The Bishop of Rome hath no jurisdiction in this Realm of England", Article XXXVII of the XXXIX Articles of Religion.

I've been to Rome only once, quite a few years ago. I was there with Miles, whom many of you will know. Initially, I refused to go into St. Peter's, citing the fact that it had been built on the proceeds of Indulgences. But, having been inside, Miles came out and insisted that I must go in. So I did.

Around the inside of the enormous dome – everything in St. Peter's is enormous – are the words, in Latin, **"You are Peter, and on this rock I will build my church"**, Matthew 16:18. It's true that Peter is buried in the basilica. But of course those words are precious to the Church of Rome, because they bolster its claim to primacy.

What are we, as Protestants, to make of them? I'm willing to accept that when Jesus spoke these words to Peter, He meant them about him. But not only is there no evidence that Peter was the first Bishop of Rome, crucially, Jesus didn't say anything about extending such an accolade, **"on this rock I will build my church"**, to any specific successors.

A normal Protestant extrapolation of this verse is to apply it to the apostles' teaching, with Peter as representative of that. That's what we mean when we affirm, "I believe the One Apostolic Church." We're saying that the Church's teaching is in a line of succession that stretches back to what the apostles taught. And that teaching, of course, is embodied in the Bible. We're saying that we're a Bible-believing Church.

We don't have a gospel procession at Holy Trinity – that's where there's a procession and the gospel is read from somewhere in the centre aisle. Partly, that's because we're just not that type of church liturgically. But in addition I'm opposed to it because it seems to be often misunderstood. I've heard it explained in terms of the gospel's being taken to the middle of the congregation; a reasonable understanding, because that's what appears to be going on. Whereas, actually, the procession is meant to represent taking the gospel out into the world.

The Greek word, *apostolos* (ἀπόστολος), from which apostolic is derived, means one who is sent out: one on a mission. The Church is apostolic in that it stands in continuity with the apostles, by showing fidelity to their teaching and by being sent into the world to witness to the good news that Jesus Christ is Lord of all; **"to bring all things in heaven and earth together under one head, even Christ"**, Ephesians 1:10. This is what it means for the Church to be *apostolic.* We talk a lot about the church gathered on Sunday morning, but let us not forget about the Church scattered throughout the remainder of the week.

"I believe the One Church" is mirrored when we affirm, "I acknowledge one Baptism for the remission of sins." It's remarkable that despite the differences between the various Christian denominations, and the fact, for example, that the Roman Catholic Church won't allow members of other Churches to receive Communion, nor will it let Roman Catholics receive Communion elsewhere, despite all that, we all acknowledge the validity of each Church's baptism.

At the Reformation, people who then found themselves in the new Protestant Churches weren't baptised; they couldn't be, because they had already been baptised, even though it had been under the auspices of Rome; this principle being encapsulated in Article XXVI of the XXXIX Articles of Religion.

The exception to this were the Anabaptists, who re-baptised, hence being given a deprecatory name meaning re-baptisers. But these precursors of modern-day Baptists were very much on the edge of the Reformation, and indeed were persecuted for being so.

We can believe the one, holy, catholic and apostolic Church only if we first believe in God the Father, God the Son, and God the Holy Spirit. At its most fundamental level the Church is a reality that is created and sustained by God – not by us. It is because each of us has been united with Jesus by the Holy Spirit, and drawn into the life of God the Father, that we are able to believe in one, holy, catholic and apostolic Church.

We believe the Church is one because we have been united with one another in Christ by one baptism. We believe the Church is catholic because the Holy Spirit draws diverse people from different places throughout time to be part of it. We believe the Church is holy because Jesus has purified it by His life, death and resurrection; it is **"a radiant church, without stain or wrinkle, or any other blemish, but holy and blameless"**, Ephesians 5:27. We believe the Church is apostolic because just as the Father has sent the Son and the Spirit into the world, we have been commissioned by Jesus in the power of the Holy Spirit to **"go into all the world and to preach the gospel** (the good news given to the apostles) **to all creation"**, [Mark 16:15].

Amen.

VIII: THE CHRISTIAN HOPE Part I (Priscilla Turner)

Texts: Gen. 3; Rom. 8:28-39; Mt. 22:1-14.

Προσδοκῶ ἀνάστασιν νεκρῶν, καὶ ζωὴν τοῦ μέλλοντος αἰῶνος.

"I expect the resurrection of dead persons, and the life of the coming age."

The story is told of the man who went to the psychiatrist complaining of high anxiety; and when asked what he did for a living, replied, "I sort potatoes into big and little: decisions, decisions!!!" Well, when you and I come up for judgement, that will be the ultimate sorting, the ultimate comeuppance. Since antiquity the smart money has always been on death futures. All but the very last generation will die. As the Christian leader said to those who, arriving at the conference centre, gathered that there were more people than beds, "Behold, brethren, I tell you a mystery: we shall not all sleep"! But, according to the New Testament, judgement futures too are a sure thing. All, dead or alive, will stand trial; and the Judge will have, not just the last word on what kind of potato I am, fit for life or only for condemnation, but the only word. Of the four possible human attitudes in the face of this, assurance, complacency, dread and denial, only two are realistic, and only one provides hope. There will be no spectators' gallery. I shall not be doing any judging: my opinion, of myself or anyone else, will not count. We can know that the Judge will be perfectly just, perfectly merciful; but we will not be consulted about what justice and mercy may mean in the case of any individual. Unless I am very far gone in pride, vainglory and hypocrisy, that fact ought to be a tremendous relief to my mind.

The Christian hope is not “Pie in the sky when you die, (and a slice for me if I feel like it)”, the old sneer of the prosperous at the simple faith of the poor. It is not for the complacent, sure that the love of God is a soft thing, who are perhaps the majority of the reasonably prosperous in our West Coast society. It has always been for those who live in the real world. It was a cold, brutal world into which the Gospel and the Creeds came. Huge numbers of people were owned as slaves, body and soul. The free remainder had better take care to be male and adult, if they hoped for any dignity or respect as of right. Dad could execute you if he didn’t happen to take a shine to you that morning. Females of all ages went from hand to hand like bits of coinage. Life was generally “solitary, poor, nasty, brutish and short”. Hope was at a premium. If you believed in the gods at all, you couldn’t think of them as worth worshipping. The Stoic hoped to be brave, the Epicurean to “eat, drink and be merry, for tomorrow we die”, the Platonist that his soul might transmigrate to a better body next time. History was cyclical and had no purpose; certainly there was no benign will behind the forces of nature. Most people lived lives of quiet desperation, attempting to console themselves with sex, drink and often violent entertainments. Huge numbers of people had no choices, and worse still bore the scars of having been torn violently apart from parents, spouse, children and their homeland. Does this remind you of anywhere you know?

In this context the Christian Faith represented the solution, not an extra burden or an intellectual puzzle in a hard and ultimately hopeless life.

I first preached this sermon in 2011. I had had quite a few weeks to meditate on today's subject. This was perhaps a mistake, in that each day I found that, like our faith as a whole, it got bigger, broader, deeper and more majestic. It is in fact as big as the New Testament. It proved impossible to do it justice in the time allotted for a Sunday sermon. So the then-Rector and I divided it into two. For our current series I hope to come on again before Easter, with my subject then being 'The Christian Hope Part Two'.

It is often said that love was the obvious characteristic of believers in the early centuries. Yes, but not subjectively: they did not sit around congratulating themselves on how loving they had become. Rather they had hope, even in bitter circumstances which could never be altered. This was how they made sense of their experience. How then may we make the same sense, and have the same assurance? Who is it that can look forward to joy not misery in the world to come? What is the significance of our transitory earthly life, and am I "just a passin' through"? I turn for answers, not modern but rooted in traditions much older than any of us, to our Gospel passage for today, which you may wish to have open now. Jesus our Lord is using a parable. This means that He is giving us a comparison or picture. As we shall see, this one is a moving picture.

Jesus said: **"The Kingdom of Heaven".** What is that? Simply put, it is the sphere in this world and the next where God is God. It is the Garden of Gen. 3, with its perfect trust and love, restored. Human beings not in it are the exiles from Eden, the out-of-tune instruments in a vast orchestra, the out-of-step dancers in the Great Dance.

" ... is like a certain king". We enter the Kingdom by returning to the King. It is because we sinners see the world through a great distorting bubble of man-centred vanity that we do not see God as He is, that is as sovereign over the dance of atoms, over every cell in our bodies. If God is King, we should constantly be going to the top with prayer and thanksgiving, trusting that though we may often be confused between our felt wants and our real needs, things are in hand however it may seem. He is personal, relational, loving and good, as I said several weeks ago.

" ... who prepared a wedding-banquet for his son". God is giving a party, a Royal Wedding with all the trimmings.

" ... and sent his servants to those who had been invited to the banquet ...". This is the two-stage oriental invitation, the only kind which is taken seriously to this day in Arab lands: first a broad "Yes" is asked for, then when the tables are laid – a big job, as feasting will go on for days – the guests are told that now's the time.

"... but they refused to come". So – the height of bad manners – they say, "But then again, maybe I won't." We see that we human beings are free to choose. We can say "No" to God. It is a personal, very personal invitation and response. Nobody can say "Yes" for us, nobody can take this freedom from us.

"Then he sent some more servants, and said, 'Tell those who have been invited that I have prepared my dinner; my oxen and my fattened cattle have been butchered, and everything is ready; come to the wedding banquet'". This shows that God is pressing and persistent in offering His welcome. He comes near to beseeching the people to come: "You should try it, you might like it".

"But they paid no attention, and went off, one to his field, another to his business". They had better things to do, and off they went to those better things, things which seemed really serious. Notice that there is nothing wrong in principle with what they did prefer: farming and commerce are good, worthy and necessary things. It's just that they would still have been there after the party: they could wait; which surely shows that at bottom the people just didn't want to go. It's quite certain, I believe, that they could have had all this and Heaven too; but with their priorities, in the end they lost the things of this world, as was bound to happen, and had nothing after them either. To quote William Law, "If you have not chosen the Kingdom of God first, it will in the end make no difference what you have chosen instead". As the man said when asked what some tycoon had left when he died, "Everything". We are what we eat, they say. Much more fundamentally, we are what we think, what we concentrate on, set our hearts on, desire most deeply, take our joy in. We used when I was young to laugh at the description of the Christian who was "so heavenly minded that he was no earthly good". Not then, and not at any time since, have I detected that that was my danger.

"The rest seized his servants, and mistreated them, and killed them". It seems that Our Lord is speaking here of a kind of people who haven't even the excuse of taking other occupations more seriously: they go out of their way to insult God and are maximally hostile to His messengers. Incidentally I find it very interesting that in these few words we have a complete account of what evangelism is. The invitation is issued from Person to person by God, but He chooses to use earthen vessels to carry it; in the process the messenger may get first hurt and then shot. I notice that no servant is authorised to leave anyone out. He will need to be gentle, forgiving, peaceable and gracious at all times. Let's watch that we too commend the Gospel not only with our lips but in our lives.

"The king was enraged; and he sent his army, and destroyed those murderers and burned their city. Then he said to his servants, 'The wedding is ready, but those I invited did not deserve to come.'" Overreaction, we might say, but this is a command invitation which has been despised, and the *lèse majesté* has been compounded by gratuitous murder. Undoubtedly the historical background to this is the rejection of God's open invitation by His ancient people, Israel, their maltreatment of a whole succession of prophets, and the coming doom of the nation and destruction of Jerusalem at the hands of Rome. But let's think for a moment what kind of people these were. Like most of us, they had every advantage from the point of view of faith. They were born and brought up as members of God's people. They thought that God's welcome was so automatic that they despised it. It is not automatic: if, for instance, you never make the baptismal promises your own, God will not receive you at the end by some kind of magic. Even the obviously pious can really be saying, "Thanks, but no thanks".

"'So go to the street corners and invite to the banquet anyone you find.' So the servants went out into the streets, and gathered all the people they could find, the bad as well as the good; and the wedding hall was filled with guests". So who does get in? Pretty much anybody else who really wants to, it seems. We shouldn't be surprised if we find the Church a mixed bunch, with a lot of imperfect characters. This is what the Kingdom looks like. Accepting our personal invitation is one thing: it can be quite a shock when we come up against the social dimension. Some of our experiences of church life can leave us not too enthusiastic about the idea of more of the same, prolonged indefinitely for all eternity. But I'm afraid there's no getting around it: Heaven will be very social. John Mason Neale, in his translation 'Jerusalem the Golden', was only literal when he wrote originally, "I know not, O I know not / What *social* joys are there". Meanwhile, we do not help ourselves if we expect smooth sailing, in this or other respects. Some people teach that the truly spiritual go through life grinning from ear to ear. That is a childish fancy, credible if you are young and strong, with a good digestive system and plenty to put in it, but it doesn't stand up to mature experience. The falsehood, last time I heard Billy Graham, was parodied by him as "Come to Christ and be healthy, wealthy and happy all your days – and please send me all your money". After the laughter had died away he added very quietly, "That is not the teaching of the New Testament". No, we must learn that eudaemonism, to use the old name – modern names are Christian Science or Prosperity Theology – is false. Joy is not the same as happiness, and in this life not all hopes are realised, all loves consummated, all enigmas solved, all injustices righted, all sorrows comforted, all illnesses made better. My dear husband's Parkinson's was not cured. It is my experience that we begin to find out what it means to rejoice in the Lord when everything else in the way of happiness has been stripped from us.

Some Christians get very excited about the Last Days, and whether they and the Lord's return are near. This is actually quite straightforward: we have been in the last days since Jesus rose from the dead, and He returns for each of us at our death, with the exception of that last generation whose 'pre-need' funeral packages will prove to be money wasted. All down the ages God's company have been collecting – what people we have met and will meet! – because He wanted them in His house. Then comes the great moment, when He is present in person: let's hope we're not caught out. In nearly 51 years of wedded bliss I have learnt a thing or two about the differences between men and women; and one of them is that for any big social occasion, the male of the species will tend to under-, the female to over-dress. Some 59 years ago my husband-then-to-be got turned away of a summer's evening from the Vienna Opera House because he had no tie on. But this is not just any social occasion, however big. Imagine the biggest bash ever, the Royal Wedding, the Coronation, the P.N.E., Expo, the Olympics, V.E. Day, the marathon run through the Brandenburg Gate, you name it, all rolled into one, magnify it a zillion times, and you have some idea of the Kingdom of Heaven in its fullness, the kind of party God wants us to be at. Is this a "Come-as-you-are" kind of thing? What *do* you wear, and how can you afford it?

"But when the King came in to see the guests, he noticed a man there who was not wearing wedding clothes. He asked, 'Friend (notice God's absolute goodwill expressed here)**, how did you get in here without wedding clothes?'"** How indeed, when they would have offered him the right stuff at the door? God's servants are supposed to be informed about appropriate dress, even if, fascinatingly, none of them had the right to turn him away for not looking right. What's going on? What has he done wrong? Tried Grandpa's best suit or something? Did he perhaps say to them, "I *came*, didn't I, and I gave up a lot to do it. I'm a busy man. Quite an imposition, an invitation like that."? Or "Of course I'm royalist in principle, but I don't believe in making a fuss of royalty, I never have, I've never fancied getting up close and personal with that family, I just came on the off-chance, for the promised food and drink."? Or "I love mankind, it's people I can't stand! Look at that bunch in there, types who have made money as abortionists, tortured people in prison, starved women and children by hoarding, profiteering, pushing up costs by their own overeating, consumed much and produced nothing at all! I even see my abusive father, whom I can't forgive! I want justice! Jean-Paul Sartre was right, hell is other people!"? One assumes that they didn't let him in with "Oh, the King's an old softie at heart, he'll make an exception for someone like you, go on in." Perhaps they said to him, "You know, there's quite a file on you too, there is on all of us, and there are people already in there who have had to forgive you for things, the little lies and cruelties that changed someone's life for the worse, the times that you said about someone what you wouldn't say to his face, the neglect and omission, some that you've forgotten, some that you never even noticed; and then there are all those for whom you made it hard to believe in the Son or His Father; there are the little ones, even the helpless animals, for whom you stood in the place of the King, and you misrepresented Him; there are those who have wanted to say to you, the monarchist, 'What you are speaks so loud that I can't hear what you say!': for pity's sake take the priceless coverall that's here for you, it's expected! Mercy's much surer than justice any day. And chances are you won't feel half as hurt and angry once you've got it on." And he replied, "Thanks but no thanks, I'm much too big for your crude one-size-fits-all stuff, I prefer to stand on my character and record!"

"The man was speechless." The question leaves him speechless. He seems not to have a clue that he wasn't OK in there just as he was. **"Then the king told the attendants, 'Tie him hand and foot** (no more freedom of choice or action) **and throw him outside** (banishment from God's presence)**, and into the darkness** (exclusion from the great company and the absence of God)**, where there will be weeping and gnashing of teeth** (bitter, bitter regret and a sense of irrevocable loss)**. For many are invited, but few chosen'".** It seems there are those who will be found at judgement day to have been in the Church but not of it. It seems that there is such a thing as perdition, final and absolute, whether or not that is the extinction of the personality or a conscious experience infinitely prolonged. And in spite of God's invitation, and the wedding clothes that He provides in the righteousness of Christ, some choose it.

Everywhere it is taught that real life starts now, and that what is central to me now (or here) will be central to me then (and there). Can I pray, **"*Thy* kingdom come, *Thy* will be done..."**? As rational adults, we either have, or have not, died to sin. Am I still the centre of my universe, or have I asked Jesus Christ to displace me and move into the centre? The medievals had an expression for the condition of the sin-sick person, *incurvatus in se ipsum,* bent inwards into himself. Do

I strive to live turned outwards to Him and my neighbour, or have I not yet started my spiritual convalescence? I need to be perfectly clear that if I have not been converted into a life of love, I have not been converted at all. God is easy to please, with just a little turning, but hard to satisfy. Is my will set to pursue virtue? We either do, or do not, live the Resurrection life today. What if I should die tonight? Am I, and have I, forgiven? My mother made us sing 'Rock of Ages' for her funeral in 1996. When at the height of my drug-withdrawal, not many months later, I was afraid of not waking up in the morning, and was asking, "What will happen to me if the next stop is Your Judgement?", I 'sang' the words to the Lord every night for quite a few nights, in the darkness, until sleep came. "A state of grace" is what it's about.

What must people like ourselves, bad characters with a mixed record, do in order to be acceptable at the only party worth going to? Only two kinds of people will I believe enjoy the new life in the Resurrection, the innocent and the forgiven, who will also be the forgiving. And perhaps additionally some who would have embraced forgiveness if it had ever been offered to them [Mt. 25:31 ff.]. Not character, but relationship is the key, not the perfection, but the direction of our life. May God give us the light and grace we need to say "Yes" to the joy of His company, and mean it, to know where to get the right clothing, and to put it on, while there is still time.

My soul, there is a country,
  Far beyond the stars,
Where stands a wingèd sentry,
  All skillful in the wars.

There, above noise and danger,
  Sweet Peace sits crowned with smiles,
And One born in a manger
  Commands the beauteous files.

He is thy gracious Friend
  And (O my soul, awake!)
Did in pure love descend,
  To die here for thy sake.

If thou canst get but thither,
  There grows the flower of peace,
The rose that cannot wither,
  Thy fortress, and thy ease.

Leave, then, thy foolish ranges;
  For none can thee secure
But One, Who never changes,
  Thy God, thy Life, thy Cure.

(*Peace* Henry Vaughan 1621–1695)

IX: THE CHRISTIAN HOPE Part II (Priscilla Turner)

Texts: Gen. 3; I Cor. 13; Mk. 10:17-31.

Προσδοκῶ ἀνάστασιν νεκρῶν, καὶ ζωὴν τοῦ μέλλοντος αἰῶνος.

"I expect the resurrection of dead persons, and the life of the coming age."

So here we go again. The story is told of a certain great and famous Cambridge New Testament scholar that having finished lecturing in June, he started up again in October with the words, "Hence it appears that …"! Well, I am not Sir Edwyn Hoskins, and it's still Lent, so I will be merciful to you, and summarise what we learnt in The Christian Hope Part One a fortnight ago, when my text was the Parable of the Great Supper in Mt. 22. Firstly, what we sinners hope for is entirely the gift of a God who is personal, relational, loving and good. Every one of us who does not belong to the last generation will "go down to dusty death". Every one of us will come up for judgement. Of the four possible human attitudes in the face of this, assurance, complacency, dread and denial, only two are realistic, and only one provides hope. Enjoyment of the best party that ever was is by invitation only. We can turn that invitation down, we can say Yes but not mean it, and we can miss it because we are not clothed in the righteousness of

Christ. Three kinds of persons only get in, the innocent, those who have never been shown the front door, which has a cross over it, so need a back door to heaven[4], and the forgiven, who will also always be the forgiving. Those who have been shown the front door, but prefer to go round to the back of the house, will find no way in, just a blank wall. The party starts now in this mortal life; if there are indeed deathbed conversions, we shouldn't count on having one. My dear father, who ministered all his working life in the Church of England, and held the hands of many people as they passed over, testified to me that he had never seen one. People generally reach the point where, in spite of dread and helpful exhortation, they are no longer capable of repentance.

The Spring before I first preached this sermon in 2011, I walked in Cambridge with my husband, as I feared for the last time. That dearest of places is by now so full of ghosts, my uncle, my first cousin once removed, my first fiancé, my lover (a reference which is fully explained in my now-published book), our best man, my father, my mother, surely an honorary Cambridge man if ever there was one, and now my husband, all people who died in Christ, all are gone. Shall I have the heart to go back there alone? For me this time it is not "if my husband were to die", but "now that my husband is dead". It's no longer parents and teachers who die, but friends and con-

---

[4] The reality of which I believe with several of the Church Fathers is the teaching of Mt. 25:31 ff.

temporaries, spouses and siblings. Time is getting so short: the people I shall never speak to about Christ, the prayers I shall never pray, the forgiveness that I cannot now ask for, the forgiveness that I have perhaps still not granted from the heart, the broken relationships that I cannot repair, the lists get longer as I get older, the burden of them is intolerable. If ever I was indifferent to the mode of our life in the world to come, and to the question of whether I shall partake of it, I am so no longer.

What can we say with certainty about life in the new heavens and new earth? By definition we mortals have no experience of the geography, topography and furniture, only the simile, metaphor and picture-language of which the New Testament is full. Pictures range from ideas of process and consummation, the prize at the end of a race, victory after battle, peace in the promised land after pilgrimage, now versus then, to spatial metaphors suggesting that heaven is a kind of place, here versus there, a glorious city, a safe pasture, a massed choir in a huge auditorium, even a vast hotel where they get your very own room ready in advance of your arrival. It is much more obvious what will be absent than what will be present. One thing we can say: we shall be with God, seen as He really is [I Cor. 13:12]. Trust and love for the Creator were lost before neighbour-love, and both before immortality. The essence of that life must be restoration of what was lost in the Garden, an unclouded trust and love between God and His creatures. We shall be with God, our suspicion, guilt and anger, our hatred done away. From that will flow an unclouded trust and love for one another. Uncorrupt, we will be fit to eat of the tree of life and so live for ever. We may expect no more conflict between duty and desire, prayer and service, activity and contemplation, zeal and tenderness, rules and warmth, self-preservation and self-giving, power and vulnerability, creativity and modesty, worship and original thought, aspiration and reality, what we seem and what we are.

There will be no trace of evil or sin. It may be that all our work will be accounted worthless: those who belong to Christ cannot be condemned as unacceptable [Jn. 6], and I know that some of you hearing me have that assurance; but every bit of their record may be good for nothing but the bonfire. We may escape the burning building with less than the clothes on our backs [I Cor. 3:10-15].

There will be no more marriage as we know it [Lk. 20:34 ff.]. Where does that leave me, who hold that men are the most beautiful things that God ever made, and that a faithful, passionate Christian husband is God's best gift to woman in this world? We will be "as the angels". That must mean a life not less, but infinitely more, full of joy, excitement, colour and light, and the faculties to receive them. Thomas Aquinas postulated seven sexes, all capable of complete interpenetration. I am not yet spiritual enough to look forward with much anticipation to endless worship like what we have here, even with Johann Sebastian Bach running the music. Wouldn't it be dull? Not if it is the big idea, not just a slice of it. Not if it encompasses succession, experience and growth. Not if the light of the glory of God is broken in that brave new world as by a prism into an infinite variety of beautiful people of all races, whose stories we may listen to for ever and ever. Not if there is music to compose, hear and perform. We may, I believe, look forward at the very least to the restoration of all those people, places and things that we have loved purely in this present life; or if not, to the gift of perfect consolation.

We have only one prototype of a resurrection body. The promise is that ours will be like that [Phil. 3:21]. What then were its characteristics? We know that there was continuity and discontinuity, that it was recognisably that of the same individual who had died, that it bore the marks of His experience, that because He was probably somewhere in His mid-30s it was neither immature nor in decay, that it was supra-material rather than immaterial, that it was imperishable and not limited by walls, time and space like an earthly one. It was able to eat and drink, but did not need to. It burst from the tomb with an explosion like an earthquake, passing through solid rock: it is of course a mistake to think that the stone had to be rolled away to let Jesus out, rather than to demonstrate that the tomb was empty. However it is done, and we most certainly must avoid crude notions of the process which, for instance, make anything less than full body burial, or cremation, capable of frustrating God's design, we may be certain that it will be faultless, a perfectly adapted vehicle of our unique personality, free of all pain, defect and mutability. We shall see fused together in countless examples youthful beauty and a mature mind. We shall see the beautiful persons of all those for whom the Creator had no plans in this world, the spontaneously and surgically aborted, those who starved to death in infancy; the brain-damaged, maimed, wounded and deformed; Jeryl will see light, colour and texture, we elderly will hear perfectly, John will walk freely, Bob and Chris who both died of Parkinson's will be steady and coordinated.

Before I go any further, I want to give you a little diagram. Imagine a square divided into four. The top left area is cross-hatched in one direction, the top right in the opposite. The bottom left area is crosshatched in both directions, the bottom right is blank. The top left area represents those aspects of our personality which are known to ourselves but not to others. The top right represents those which are known to others but not to ourselves. The bottom left represents those which are known to others as well as to ourselves. The bottom right represents those which are known only to God.

How may we get assurance, as opposed to a naïve wish-fulfilment complacency? For this I believe that we must look at our Gospel reading in Mark 10.

17 As Jesus started on his way, a man ran up to him and fell on his knees before him. "Good teacher," he asked, "what must I do to inherit eternal life?"

This kind of all-encompassing question was the regular challenge to any would-be Rabbi. Sometimes when put to Jesus it was sincere. To inherit is to get a piece of eternal life for oneself, in other words get to heaven.

18 "Why do you call me good?" Jesus answered. "No one is good – except God alone.

Because Jesus did accept reverence like this in other contexts, his reply is a little mysterious. Perhaps He was trying to head the man off from an insincere, histrionic grand gesture.

19 You know the commandments: 'You shall not murder, you shall not commit adultery, you shall not steal, you shall not give false testimony, you shall not defraud, honour your father and mother.'"

Can He say that to us? These rules, the ethical clauses of the Ten Commandments, are the basic minimum. St. Paul, with whose young self some have identified this man, states this quite plainly in Rom. 13:8 ff. Because we so easily deceive ourselves about what love is, we cannot dispense with them in this life. They function a bit like the mould to the Jell-O, supplying shape and definition: you can't eat the mould, but without it you are unlikely to get any Jell-O.

20 "Teacher," he declared, "all these I have kept since I was a boy."

That is a very good record of love for neighbour. This man has functioned on a much higher level of godliness than many modern professing Christians. Not for him the worship of Aphrodite, the goddess of sexual orgasm, expressed in pre- or extra-marital physical relations, nor the cult of Bacchus, God of escapist intoxication. The one true God had knocked such worship out of the minds of the people of Israel many centuries before. Have we submitted to the same re-education? Do we pollute our minds and bodies with any form of unchastity, the viewing, making and purveying of pornography, or dependence on any form of chemical toxin? This First Century Jew understands among other things the keeping of promises, transparency in business, the protection of his neighbour's life, property and reputation. A society full of people with such a record is both happy and stable.

21 Jesus looked at him and loved him.

This can mean only that He approved, even admired him. He is very like Jesus. Father, Son and Holy Spirit, they all want righteousness out of us. Without it we are not in the heavenly way.

"One thing you lack," he said.

Jesus also knows him. God is easy to please, but hard to satisfy. Money can feed the illusion that it is possible to do enough, for both God and neighbour. Money may not buy happiness, but it certainly buys many things that conduce to it. As the disciples point out in their bewilderment, it can buy immunity to many temptations. They perhaps hadn't seen, with their less advanced technology, anything quite like the glossy magazine that I once saw in a dentist's waiting-room, with, I kid you not, the one-word title 'Self'. Money can buy an excellent record. No need to look elsewhere if you've had enough to marry the girl of your dreams, no need to engage in corruption or sharp practice, to evade taxes, to tear others down in order to enhance your reputation. One thing money certainly cannot buy, and that is immunity to idolatry, of money and self. That this was many people's trouble is clear from the emphasis in our Lord's teaching in the gospel record. Everything old is new again. But the old pagan gods were dead in Palestinian Judaism, a sufficient explanation of why questions of sex-ethics, apart from new wives for old, scarcely figure: they were completely closed.

"Go, sell everything you have and give to the poor, and you will have treasure in heaven. Then come, follow me."

It is important to understand that it is not a sin to be rich, provided the riches are not ill-gotten. The Lord is not enunciating a moral platitude with a Marxist twist. Not all the wealthy must divest themselves of their wealth for the sake of holiness. That would let most of us out. But for this man his wealth was his sticking-point. For most of us, if we have one, it is something different. That's not to say that we can be complacent even about wealth, if for instance when we hear of bloody revolution in an oil-producing country our first thought is not the welfare of the people but the price of oil. Jesus' challenge is perhaps to our pride in physical beauty, in academic achievement, in career distinction, in social position or race, even in our poverty and work for the poor. What or whom that we really loved have we ever given up for Jesus Christ? Is there something that stands between you and really belonging to Him, that you need to divest yourself of? If we lack assurance that we are in the heavenly way, we need to identify our sticking-point, and surrender our idolatry, not with some flamboyant gesture, but from the heart. Otherwise we will find out the hard way that if you fight Jesus, Jesus will win.

22 At this the man's face fell. He went away sad, because he had great wealth.

This person had come to Jesus with everything but what he really needed. He left in the same condition, because the price was too high. What had he really wanted? All this and heaven too, bought with his fine record plus a little conventional alms-giving? Painless tithing, for him powerless to root out greed and covetousness from the heart? Not it seems real love for God and neighbour.

23 Jesus looked around and said to his disciples, "How hard it is for the rich to enter the kingdom of God!"

Does anyone according to the Bible go to perdition for what he does not know? I believe not. Is all Our Lord's teaching on perdition addressed to the earnestly but blindly religious? Yes, perhaps it is. Is Hell, if it lasts for ever, what Heaven feels like to those who are not comfortable in God's company? That is an old and to me helpful idea. It would be the agony of warm sun, but no skin to feel with, wonderful dinner smells, but no mouth to eat with, glorious surroundings, but no eyes to see with, splendid company and music, but no ears to hear with, endless speeches, and libraries full of books, all in an impenetrable language, friendly people but no arms to reach out with, and all this with no way back, no way home. Sadness indeed.

My topic, if really adequately handled, is so huge that it would take three days and three nights to begin to deal with it. There's a sense in which there is no other subject in the New Testament, and that's what you should read to get a real handle on it. I debated just reading to you C.S. Lewis' great sermon 'The Weight of Glory', simply the best. The best-known part of it reads like this: "There are no ordinary people. You have never talked to a mere mortal. Nations, cultures, arts, civilisations – these are mortal, and their life is to ours as the life of a gnat. But it is immortals whom we joke with, work with, marry, snub, and exploit – immortal horrors or everlasting splendours. This does not mean that we are to be perpetually solemn. We must play. But our merriment must be of the kind (and it is, in fact, the merriest kind) which exists between people who have, from the outset, taken each other seriously – no flippancy, no superiority, no presumption. And our charity must be real and costly love, with deep feeling for the sins in spite of which we love the sinners – no mere tolerance, or indulgence which parodies love as flippancy parodies merriment. Next to the Blessed Sacrament itself, your neighbour is the holiest object presented to your senses. If he is your Christian neighbour, he is holy in almost the same way, for in him also Christ *vere latitat*, the glorifier and the glorified, Glory Himself, is truly hidden." Much else of Lewis is profoundly relevant, and I commend it to you.

Particularly in the days and weeks after losing to death some much-loved Christian person, what does it mean that I have a vivid sense of that person's care and prayers for me, as though they had already passed through judgement and resurrection? Certain it is, I believe, that the blessed dead hold nothing against us. Why do we speak of someone's having already "gone to glory" or being "at rest in heaven"? Are there, as theologians have sometimes said (I recall presiding over a meeting of my College Classical Society in 1959, when I had invited C.S. Lewis, and he gave a paper on 'Time in Boethius'), several different kinds of time? I'm asking you to tell me.

What does all this mean for us, today and tomorrow, if the Lord tarry and we are spared? It means that we can get our priorities straight. In this perspective we shall get our earthly desires into balance: we never need to smash and grab for more and more enjoyment in this life, as though there were nothing but emptiness beyond it. The fine art and the places that I shall never see, the music that I shall never hear, the books I shall never read, the people I shall never meet in this world, all these I can relax about. If we have prayed instead of going shopping, worked instead of reading something amusing, evangelised instead of talking about ourselves, abstained instead of stuffing our face, what have we lost? In fact, according to His word in today's Gospel, the more we have surrendered for Christ here, the more we shall have there, and it will last for ever.

EVEN such is Time, that takes in trust
Our youth, our joys, our all we have,
And pays us but with earth and dust;
Who in the dark and silent grave,
When we have wander'd all our ways,
Shuts up the story of our days;
But from this earth, this grave, this dust,
My God shall raise me up, I trust.

(*The Conclusion* Sir Walter Raleigh 1552-1618)

TEXTS AND BIBLIOGRAPHY

1. *THE ORIGINAL TEXT OF THE NICENE CREED*

Πιστεύομεν εἰς ἕνα Θεόν, Πατέρα, Παντοκράτορα, ποιητὴν οὐρανοῦ καὶ γῆς, ὁρατῶν τε πάντων καὶ ἀοράτων.
Καὶ εἰς ἕνα Κύριον Ἰησοῦν Χριστόν, τὸν Υἱὸν τοῦ Θεοῦ τὸν μονογενῆ, τὸν ἐκ τοῦ Πατρὸς γεννηθέντα πρὸ πάντων τῶν αἰώνων·
φῶς ἐκ φωτός, Θεὸν ἀληθινὸν ἐκ Θεοῦ ἀληθινοῦ, γεννηθέντα οὐ ποιηθέντα, ὁμοούσιον τῷ Πατρί, δι' οὗ τὰ πάντα ἐγένετο.
Τον δι' ἡμᾶς τοὺς ἀνθρώπους καὶ διὰ τὴν ἡμετέραν σωτηρίαν κατελθόντα ἐκ τῶν οὐρανῶν καὶ σαρκωθέντα
ἐκ Πνεύματος Ἁγίου καὶ Μαρίας τῆς Παρθένου καὶ ἐνανθρωπήσαντα.
Σταυρωθέντα τε ὑπὲρ ἡμῶν ἐπὶ Ποντίου Πιλάτου, καὶ παθόντα καὶ ταφέντα.
Καὶ ἀναστάντα τῇ τρίτῃ ἡμέρᾳ κατὰ τὰς Γραφάς.
Καὶ ἀνελθόντα εἰς τοὺς οὐρανοὺς καὶ καθεζόμενον ἐκ δεξιῶν τοῦ Πατρός.
Καὶ πάλιν ἐρχόμενον μετὰ δόξης κρῖναι ζῶντας καὶ νεκρούς, οὗ τῆς βασιλείας οὐκ ἔσται τέλος.
Καὶ εἰς τὸ Πνεῦμα τὸ Ἅγιον, τὸ κύριον, τὸ ζωοποιόν,
τὸ ἐκ τοῦ Πατρὸς ἐκπορευόμενον,
τὸ σὺν Πατρὶ καὶ Υἱῷ συμπροσκυνούμενον καὶ συνδοξαζόμενον,
τὸ λαλῆσαν διὰ τῶν προφητῶν.
Εἰς μίαν, Ἁγίαν, Καθολικὴν καὶ Ἀποστολικὴν Ἐκκλησίαν.
Ὁμολογῶ ἓν βάπτισμα εἰς ἄφεσιν ἁμαρτιῶν.
Προσδοκῶ ἀνάστασιν νεκρῶν.
Καὶ ζωὴν τοῦ μέλλοντος αἰῶνος.

Ἀμήν.

2. THE TWO CREEDS WHICH WE SAY REGULARLY[5]

(a) THE APOSTLES' CREED:	(b) THE NICENE/ CHALCEDONIC CREED:
(1) I *believe in God the Father, Ruler of all, Maker of heaven and earth;*	(1) We *believe in* one *God the Father, Ruler of all, Maker of heaven and earth* and of all things seen and unseen;
(2) *and in Jesus Christ*	(2) *and in* one *Lord Jesus Christ*
His *only Son* our *Lord.*	the *only*-begotten *Son* of God begotten by the Father before all worlds, God from God, Light from Light, true God from true God, begotten not made, having the identical nature as the Father; through Him (the Son) all things were made. For us men and for our salvation *He* came down from heaven,
He was conceived *through the Holy Spirit,* born *from the Virgin Mary,*	and was enfleshed *through the Holy Spirit from the Virgin Mary,* and was made human.
suffered under Pontius Pilate, He was crucified, dead *and buried.*	*He was crucified* also for us *under Pontius Pilate,* He *suffered and was buried.*

[5] Material which is verbally identical is in Italics.

He descended to the dead.	
***The third day He rose again* from the dead.**	***The third day He rose again* in accordance with the Scriptures**
He ascended into heaven, and is seated at the right hand of the Father.	***He ascended into heaven, and is seated at the right hand of the Father.***
He will come again to judge the living and the dead.	***He will come again* with glory *to judge the living and the dead.***
	His kingdom shall have no end.
(3) I *believe in the Holy Spirit,*	**(3) We *believe in the Holy Spirit,***
	the Lord, the Giver of life, Who issues from the Father (and the Son)[6], **and with the Father is worshipped and glorified, and Who spoke through the Prophets.**
the *holy catholic church,*	**And we believe one *holy catholic* and apostolic *church.***
the communion of saints,	
the forgiveness of sins,	**I acknowledge one baptism for *the forgiveness of sins.***
***the resurrection of* the body,**	**And I expect *the resurrection of* dead persons,**
***and the life* everlasting.**	***and the life* of the coming age.**

[6] The *filioque* clause.

3. A BRIEF BIBLIOGRAPHY (a) light (b) medium (c) heavy:

(a)

Packer, J.I. *I Want to be a Christian.* 1977 (newer title *Growing in Christ*).

McGrath, Alister. *I Believe.* 1991.

Sayers, Dorothy L. *The Emperor Constantine.* 1951.

Simcox, Carroll E. *Living the Creed.* 1954.

Stott, John R.W. *Your Confirmation.* Second ed. 1993.

(b)

Bray, Gerald. *Creeds, Councils and Christ.* 1984.

(c)

Bray, Gerald. 'The *Filioque* Clause in History and Theology'. *TB* 34 (1983) pp. 91-144.

Bruce, F.F. *The Canon of Scripture.* 1988.

Frend, W.H.C. *The Rise of Christianity.* 1984.

Kelly, J.N.D. *Early Christian Creeds.* Third ed. 2006.

Early Christian Doctrines. Fifth rev. ed. 2000.

Kinzig, Wolfram. *Faith in Formulae: A Collection of Early Christian Creeds and Creed-related Texts* (4 Volumes). 2017.

Robinson, J.A.T. *Redating the New Testament.* 1976.

Almighty and everlasting God, who hast given us thy servants grace by the confession of a true faith to acknowledge the glory of the eternal Trinity, and in the power of the Divine Majesty to worship the Unity: keep us steadfast in this faith, and evermore defend us in all adversities; who livest and reignest, one God, world without end.

Amen.

Printed in the USA
CPSIA information can be obtained
at www.ICGtesting.com
JSHW010717040624
64094JS00013B/196